BOOKER T. WASHINGTON

Educator of Hand, Head, and Heart

This is the inspiring story of a modern Moses who led his people out of bondage. Born a slave, working in fields and mines, Booker struggled for an education, and in 1872 at the age of 15 enrolled at Hampton Normal and Agricultural Institute. At the age of 22 he was commissioned to found a college for Negroes at Tuskegee, Alabama. Fighting debt all the way, Tuskegee and Dr. Washington produced teachers, carpenters, tinsmiths, farmers, and today Tuskegee is one of the most important colleges in the South. When Booker T. Washington died in 1915, his people came from all over the country to pay homage to the man who had given so generously of himself so that his people might learn to be self-sufficient.

BOOKER T. WASHINGTON

Educator of Hand, Head, and Heart

by

SHIRLEY GRAHAM

Frontispiece and Jacket
by Donald W. Lambo

JULIAN MESSNER   *New York*

Published by Julian Messner
Division of Pocket Books, Inc.
8 West 40th Street, New York 10018

© Copyright 1955 by SHIRLEY GRAHAM

Tenth Printing, 1966

Printed in the United States of America

Library of Congress Catalog Card No. 55–9855

Contents

He's burned a story in my brain,
Set in my heart a song.
He and his like, by wave and main,
World without end—and not in vain—
Are towing this world along!

—*William Rose Benét*

Part I

OUT OF SLAVERY

✧✧✧

"No race can prosper till it learns that there is as much dignity in tilling a field as in writing a poem."

—Booker T. Washington

1

Great Day in the Morning

Not even the chickens were asleep on their roost as they should be in the middle of the night. The little boy hunched against the shed could hear them clucking and pecking behind him. By the light of the fire he saw folks going in and out the cabins just as they did Sundays mornings when nobody had to go to the fields. But now there was no shouting or calling out. Whenever the whispering voices seemed to bubble over with excitement they were quickly smothered in throaty laughter. Padding feet came out of the darkness beyond the slave quarters, while from the valley along the creek he could hear singing that rose and fell in the distance.

Most amazing of all was the big chunk of meat which hung, sputtering and sizzling, over the fire in the middle of the yard. The boy's mother, Jane, was cook for the Big House. But tonight the Big House was dark and still, not a light showing. Clearly his mother was not cooking right now for the master's table! The boy shivered with anticipation. He had just burned his fingers snatching at that meat, but the juicy morsel between his teeth was well worth burning all his fingers—if need be, all his toes. Nothing so good as this had been around since the days when young Marse Billy went possum hunting—and that was long ago, before the war started. The boy had been too small then to help beat the bushes for Marse Billy, but he was close by when they roasted the possum. He remembered the slaves always had a whole possum all for themselves. He sighed, now, thinking how everybody cried when young Marse Billy was killed in the war. War was terrible! No more hunting.

11

No more good times. A black boy didn't dare go into the woods any more.

At this moment the boy's mother appeared and threw some pine cones on the fire. At sight of her shining face all unhappy thoughts disappeared. When the flames hissed and flared, the boy saw the big gray rooster, high on his perch, flap his wings and stretch his long neck as if about to crow.

" 'Tain't mornin' yet," warned the boy. "Hush yo' mouth!"

He grinned when the old rooster pecked angrily at the cross bar and then buried his head in quivering wings.

"That you, Booker?" His mother peered into the corner.

The boy wiped his hand carefully over his mouth.

"Yessum," he said.

"Lan' sakes, us thought you'd gone off to the creek with Johnny. Come 'long with me an' Mandy. All us goin' now."

"The wood's awful dark." Booker's eyes were wide with apprehension as he slowly got to his feet.

Booker's mother was always so busy in the hot kitchen cabin that he could seldom get near her. But tonight when he came out of the shadows she dropped on her knees and, throwing her arms about him, drew him so close that he could feel her heart beating against his. And her voice was like a song.

"Chile, chile," she said, "sunup's most here! This is the night to go down on our knees and praise God for His goodness. Black folks been weepin' so long—been prayin' so long. Now the day's coming—the Great Day we been waitin' for. Yo' gonna be free, son! Yo' gonna be free!"

She held him off so that she could see the small pinched face in the firelight. His skin was lighter than hers and was marred by bruises and scratches from carrying wood and struggling with heavy sacks of meal or beans. His only garment, a flax shirt, had originally belonged to his brother, John. It hung loosely almost to the knees of his scanty frame. But she noted thankfully that this younger son of hers was no weakling. The slight shoulders were square and the gray eyes staring out at her were steady and clear.

She pressed him to her again and murmured, "Thank yo', Jesus! Ma po' lil boy will be free! My children will be free!"

Only five winters had passed since this child was born. They had been long, lean seasons of strife and want. She had held this baby in her arms and trembled with fear on the night the patrol came looking for old John Brown. They searched the slave cabins, turned them upside down, and cursed every living thing on the place. All the slaves knew about that Grand Old Man, but nobody told the patrollers a thing. Afterward many slaves went off. Those left behind had to work harder and had less to eat. Among those who went was Jane's husband, Tom, who belonged to the Colbert Plantation, ten miles away. He appeared suddenly one night and told her he was running away to join the Union soldiers. "Gonna help fight for freedom," he said. Then he was gone. No word reached the plantation from any of the slaves who ran away. But now—*Mistah Lincoln was setting all the slaves free!*

There was a sound like the rustle of wind throughout the slave quarters as the cabins spilled their occupants into the night and the whispering voices mingled. Booker's mother rose to her feet.

"Wait till I get Mandy," she said quickly.

Cripple Joe hobbled out of his corner and Granny Lou came leaning on her knotted stick.

"Hit's time, chillin! Hit's time!" the old lady called in a cracked voice. Nobody tried to hush her, for Granny Lou was the oldest slave in all the county and respected by all.

"Granny," Booker's mother addressed her anxiously, "I'm 'fraid yo' can't walk so far. Why not—"

"Leave off, daughter," interrupted Granny. "Mah legs took me to see George Washington. I'm goin' now to sit me down by the watah to watch the sun rise on dis hyear day. Freedom makes me strong, daughter!"

"Amen!" said deep voices.

Booker padded along beside his mother to the cabin which was home. There small Mandy peered out the door. She was only half as big as Booker. The mother lifted the child into her arms.

"Come on, Booker," she said.

13

The boy looked back to where the large piece of meat still browned over the low fire.

"When we eat?" he asked.

There was warm, understanding laughter as the slaves made their way toward the woods. All shared Booker's interest in that succulent roast. But eating could wait until they had welcomed the Great Day.

Though lights were extinguished and all was quiet and still, not everyone was sound asleep in the Big House. Miss Anne tossed fretfully in her pretty east room. She had returned that day from a Christmas party in Roanoke. But all her favorite male cousins were away someplace with Virginia's troops. She had found her female cousins and their friends very dull indeed. On the other side of the house Jones Burroughs, Esquire, master of the plantation, shifted heavily on his bed and suppressed a deep sigh lest he waken his wife who was stretched out on her back beside him. And though the mistress lay motionless her eyes were wide open in the darkness, while every now and then a tear trickled down the side of her face.

On this last night of the year 1862 Mistress Burroughs was thinking about the son who would never come home again. Her mind went back to the Christmas when Bill had insisted on trimming the tree for the younger children. He'd been so pleased when small Chester shrieked with delight. At this the mother's heart twisted anew. For where was Chester tonight? Would he, too, be killed in the awful war? *Oh, my sons, my sons!* Pressed down as she was with grief, the mistress gave no heed to the unusual stirring in the distant slave quarters.

The master did hear and wondered what was going on. It was, however, still the Christmas season, when plantation discipline was relaxed. With only one more day free from work, the slaves were evidently bent on enjoying themselves. Until tonight the holiday had passed very quietly. The slaves could not, as formerly, go from one plantation to another eating, dancing, and drinking cheap whisky provided by the masters. War between the states had put an end to all that.

Burroughs Plantation could not be compared with rich tideland plantations in eastern Virginia, but it was one of the best in Franklin County. An inventory taken in November, 1861, accounted for wide fields, woodlands, and pastures with livestock, hogs, and chickens all tended by over a hundred able-bodied slaves. This last item, however, included many children, among whom was listed:

One small Negro boy, "Booker," value $400

When the master was asked why he set so high a value on this particular "small Negro boy," Mr. Burroughs thought a moment, then explained, "He's exceptionally bright. Furthermore, there's good blood in him."

The official recording the inventory shrugged his shoulders and grunted. This apparently bothered the master, who frowned.

"Aim to sell him off right soon, though. Never can tell how his kind will turn out."

This was all the record ever made of Booker's birth. Recently the master had been too occupied with other matters to recall his intention to get rid of the boy.

Planters knew they would be ruined if the war did not end soon. It was becoming increasingly difficult to ship anything. Bales of cotton were piling up on river landings, and tobacco was drying out in smokehouses. Every planter was losing slaves at an alarming rate—they were being encouraged to run away by the Yankees!

The master again turned uneasily on his bed. Things outside had quieted down, but now he thought he heard singing. He raised himself on his elbow and listened. Through a nearby window he could see that night was fading away, revealing trees black against a dusky sky. He could hear the singing now quite plainly. It certainly did not come from the slave quarters but from much farther away. It sounded like a large number of voices blending together in that eerie fashion of which only the slaves seemed capable. The master listened a moment and frowned. There was something disturbing about this which he could not define. Why should they leave their quarters to go off singing like this? Why—just before the dawn of New Year's Day? Could it be possible they had picked up the preposterous talk about the Yankee President freeing slaves at this time? How could that Rail Splitter take slaves away from their rightful owners by edict? *Ridiculous!* The master snorted indignantly as he lay back on his pillow. Let them sing! Tomorrow he'd see that everybody was back at work.

Nothing could have stopped the slaves' singing that morning. They had come from all the plantations for miles around, trudging through dusty roads, across broken fields, and through woods. This creek valley had been their meeting place for a long, long time. Here they had listened while the Preacher read the Word. Here they had bowed upon the ground and prayed; here they had comforted one another in sorrow, had passed secret messages, had made plans for slipping away. But never before had they gathered in such numbers; never had they come so openly; never had they lifted their voices so boldly:

"I gotta home in dat Rock,
Ain't dat good news?
I gotta home in dat Rock,
Ain't dat good news?"

They sang, swaying in unison. They sang, holding each other by the hand while the curtains of night slowly rolled back . . . while the dawn trembled just below the horizon.

Then, suddenly, above the dark, rugged line of the distant ridge a single finger of light shot upward. A hush fell over the waiting throng while the shaft widened and deepened. The body of the sky faded and the east began to glow with all the colors of the rainbow. The crowd swayed to its knees. Only the Preacher stood on a little knoll, his deeply furrowed black face raised to the sky, the ring of white hair like a halo about his head. One moment more before he lifted his hand and sent his voice like a mighty clarion ringing through the valley: "Praise God, all creatures here below! Praise God, who brings this Great Day!"

The song started with a single voice. It spread like a flame from the sun, whose rim could now be seen. The black people

16

leaped to their feet, tears of joy rolling down their upturned faces while the song rose to a mighty chorus:

> "Free at last,
> Free at last,
> Thank God Almighty,
> I'm free at last!"

Small Booker clutched his mother's skirt and heard the song pouring from her throat. His big brother, John, close beside him, also sang. Even little Mandy piped up with her voice. But Booker could not sing. The lump in his throat nearly choked him and his legs were shaking. He was glad when his mother looked down at him.

She saw his quivering face and dropped down on her knees. Thanksgiving flowed like a river from her heart as she encircled them all in her arms—John, and Mandy, and Booker—her children.

> "No more auction block for me!
> No more, no more—
> No more auction block for me!
> Many thousands gone."

◆◆◆◆◆◆◆◆◆◆◆◆◆◆◆◆◆◆ 2 ◆◆◆◆◆◆◆◆◆◆◆◆◆◆◆◆◆◆

The Long Journey

Freedom did not come all at once. Instead, following President Lincoln's Emancipation Proclamation, the whole country was plunged into bitter fighting. Slave owners were determined not to give up their slaves. More work was piled on them and severe penalties were enacted for those who ran away.

17

The war came very close to Burroughs Plantation. At night Booker lay in his corner and heard the big guns. Hidden in the thicket, he watched soldiers going by on the road. They were fierce-looking creatures with bristling hair all over their faces, their clothes stained and crusted with mud. The soldiers took every good horse and mule off the plantation until there was nothing left but a few old nags. They drove off the cows.

About this time the overseer noticed that Booker was big enough for heavier work than sweeping yards, cleaning chicken-houses, and feeding pigs.

One morning after filling the pig trough the boy paused long enough to see that all got a fair share of their feeding. One little pig, weaker and less aggressive than the rest, was usually pushed and shoved aside by the huge snorting beasts. Booker was leaning over the pigsty ready to do a little pushing on his own part when he was startled by a loud, harsh voice.

"Hey there, ye lazy scamp, leave them hogs alone! Got nothing to do but eat up the pigs' slop?" It was the big red overseer and Booker trembled with apprehension.

"Nossah! Nossah!" he gasped. "I was jus'—"

"Don't sass me, young'un," snapped the overseer. "Come along! I'm putting ye to work."

Cold chills shook the boy. His mother, brother, or some older slave had always kept him busy. Never before had he been "put to work" by the overseer himself. The slave child knew what this meant. However, there was nothing to do but follow after the big man.

"Hey, Joe!" called the overseer when he reached the barn with Booker trotting behind him. "Bring them sacks of corn! This runt can take 'em to the mill."

Cripple Joe hobbled out dragging two heavy sacks. The old man screwed up his eyes when he saw the child, but said nothing.

"Load 'em on the mare," growled the overseer. "I reckon she can make it to the mill and back."

Booker watched wide-eyed while Cripple Joe tossed the sacks over the mare's sagging back and fastened them so that one hung down on each side. He had been to the mill several

18

times with his brother. He knew the way. But to go alone—to be entrusted with so important an errand! The small slave was bewildered and frightened.

"Now up with ye, punk! Get down to the mill and have 'em grind this corn."

"Jus'—jus' me, sah?" asked Booker in a quivering voice.

"Stop whining and be off! No loiterin' on the way or I'll take the hide off yer back."

Cripple Joe lifted the boy onto the horse and started him on his way by giving the mare a sharp slap and calling, "Gittee up!"

Booker clutched the shaggy mane and tried to hold on to the reins. He was used to riding behind some good-natured worker going from one place to another on the plantation. But now, perched as he was with his legs sticking out over the bulging bags, the broad, slippery back of the mare seemed a most unstable place. Fortunately the old horse knew her way to the road. By the time they passed through the gate and were well away from the overseer's baleful voice, rider and horse felt easier. Booker wiggled his toes and remembered that *going to the mill was fun!*

The mill was three miles down the road where a tributary of the Roanoke River ran swiftly between two high narrow banks. It was a favorite meeting spot for slaves on the surrounding plantations. Sometimes there was quite a crowd calling out, talking and laughing, while each waited his turn with the miller.

"Gittee up!" Booker called out stoutly. He was anxious to get there. He was anxious to take *his* place in the line.

They reached the mill without mishap. The boy was disappointed to see so few people about the place. He got off the horse and walked boldly inside. The miller let out a big laugh when Booker announced his errand.

"Burroughs must be scraping the bottom of the barrel!" he exclaimed. "All his slaves run away, eh?"

Booker knew better than to say anything when white folks laughed, so he just backed out the door to wait for his ground

19

corn. Two black men standing near the door regarded him with interest.

"Yo' from Burroughs'?" asked one.

"Yessah," answered Booker. Children were always respectful to elders.

"Bright boy," commented the man.

"Hump!" muttered the other. "Don't be too bright!"

Booker's eyes slid over the second speaker to the big wheel. This was what he liked best of all: to watch it dip down into the water and then come up all shining and dripping and shimmering . . . then splash again.

Much too soon they called him to say that his corn was ready. One of the bystanders lifted the heavy bags and tied them on the mare. Then he lifted the boy onto the horse. Feeling very satisfied with himself, Booker started homeward.

After a long hot summer the day was pleasantly cool. Booker was gazing longingly at a big apple tree near the road when he suddenly realized something was wrong. The weight of one of the bags was pulling him off the horse! He grabbed the ropes and began to pull. But the corn had not been evenly divided. As it shifted about, the bags had become unbalanced.

"Whoa! Whoa!" the boy called.

Now the horse began to wobble. It was no use. The bags slowly slipped to the ground pulling the small boy along with them. The horse stood motionless looking down at the heap.

Booker had no time to nurse his wounds. He must get those bags back on the horse. Nothing else mattered. Tears stung his eyes as he pulled and tugged trying to reload the corn on the horse. The mare stood patiently while Booker ran from side to side, dragging, lifting, and pulling. But his reach was too short; his arms lacked the strength—he could not get the bags back in place! He looked around for help. Not a soul was in sight. And the high noon sun was sinking toward the west. He would be late getting home. The overseer would beat him! Maybe he could get help at the big place just around the bend. But dare he leave the corn? Another fear shook him. *Soldiers!* Soldiers might come along and take it! He tried again—pulled and strained until every part of his body ached. He was sobbing now, short, hard sobs that caught in his throat. It was no use. The overseer would come and beat him there in the road. The child leaned against the warm, heaving side of the old mare and cried bitterly. Then he heard wheels bumping over the road. Somebody was coming around the bend! He ran forward to meet a donkey cart driven by what might have been a scarecrow.

"Please, please, mistah!" he called. "Help me! Help me!" He stumbled and fell in the dust.

The slave in the cart recognized the little fellow. He had seen him at the mill. He saw at once what the trouble was. It was only a matter of minutes before the bags of corn were securely fastened—this time carefully balanced—and Booker was back on top the mare. For a while the donkey cart kept him company, then disappeared in a cloud of dust down a side road.

The old horse loped along at its best pace. The sun was still high in the sky when they turned into the gate. But as the boy slid to the ground in front of the barn he heard the dreaded voice.

" 'Bout time ye got back. I was just reachin' for my whip. Hey, Joe, put this here corn meal away! And ye, runt, git over to them henhouses and clean 'em out!"

Booker scampered away, thankful to escape punishment.

From this day on, Booker was sent regularly to the mill. He dreaded every trip and tried to explain about the bags slipping. But nobody listened to a tiny slave's problems. His brother, John, had been sent to the fields. He was only a few years older than Booker but already was dulled and cowed with hard work and beatings. The Big House overflowed with relatives whose home had been burned in Richmond. Booker's mother, Jane, did not have a moment she could give to her little boy.

It was up to Booker to see that the corn was evenly distributed and the bags securely fastened. From Cripple Joe he learned how this could be done. At the mill he made himself useful by filling his own bags. And when one of the men lifted them to his horse he dashed about pulling the ropes fast and tightening knots. This usually meant a safe trip home. But sometimes the miller was in a hurry and shoved the little fellow out of his way, or the load was carelessly packed on the mare. Then the bags would fall off and Booker would have to wait till a chance passer-by came along who would help him out of his trouble.

One day while he waited in fear and trembling a fierce thunderstorm blew up. It did not last long, but the corn meal was drenched through and through. A farmer rode by soon afterward and fastened the soggy bags to Booker's shivering mare. They were a sorry sight when they reached home. And the overseer flogged the terrified child unmercifully.

Afterward Booker crawled on hands and knees through the hedge surrounding the Big House. If he could only *see* his mother! Late-afternoon sun streamed over the close-cropped lawn, and the air was sweet to smell. The boy crouching in the hedge heard laughter. Peeping through the hedge, he saw three girls on the grass. They were like beautiful birds hopping about. He gazed at the starched white dresses, the golden bobbing curls, the trim, pretty little feet in shining slippers, and could scarcely breathe. The three were just about his own size. Then he saw his mother. She was coming down the porch steps carrying a big plate.

The little girls saw her, too, and one of them shouted, "Oh-oh-oh-oh-oh! Goody, goody! Look! Ginger cakes!" They danced about her clapping their hands.

Booker watched while his mother gave each of the beautiful little girls two large brown ovals—one in each hand. He watched while they bit into them . . . heard their cries of delight. Surely a ginger cake was the most delicious thing in the whole world! He watched his mother go back into the house. He crouched in the hedge until dark, but he did not see her again.

During these months the slaves could hardly have had anything to sing about. Yet often, late at night, there was singing in the slave quarters. The old folks prayed for the success of "Mistah Lincoln's soldars" and behind the overseer's back they still whispered the word "freedom." Then one morning the overseer was not there. Nobody bothered to ask when or how he left. They made certain his cabin was empty, waited until confirmation filtered down from the Big House, then rejoiced.

"Maybe the Yankees got 'im!" was one hopeful comment.

An' cut off his ears! was what Booker added in his own thoughts.

A couple of days passed and somebody came down from the Big House to take charge of things.

"Poor kin," whispered Granny Lou contemptuously.

However that may have been, it soon became apparent that "Mr. Harris" knew very little about what ought to be done on the plantation. His manner was unsure and hesitating. He did not even carry a whip. Some of the slaves went about their duties as usual. Others quite frankly "rested up for a spell." That season no cotton was taken down to the already crowded river landing. Tobacco plants were set out, but a large part of the crop rotted in the ground. Much of the land was not even plowed up.

Cripple Joe sent Booker to the mill whenever there was corn to be ground. Booker made the infrequent trips willingly enough. There was little danger now of being stranded on the road waiting for help. More people were moving about since crops were poor everywhere, markets had vanished, and all the strong men were away at war.

By this time the small boy with his corn was a familiar sight at the mill. Other slaves who came regularly grinned and called out as he slid off the bony mare. Somebody always came forward to help him with the heavy bags. And Booker enjoyed this moment of importance.

But one afternoon in early spring a group of white men gathered in front of the mill fell silent as the mare halted. Booker could feel their eyes on him and a lump came up in his throat. He strained his ears for a friendly voice. Nobody called out. Nobody laughed. The only sound was the splash and grind of the big wheel.

Keeping his eyes straight in front of him, Booker descended and with shaking fingers untied his bags. He would have to drag them right between those silent white men. What were they doing there? He turned, keeping his eyes on the ground, and started toward the entrance to the mill. A heavy hand on his shoulder nearly knocked him down.

"Whose boy you?" demanded a harsh voice.

"I Massa Burroughs' boy, sah." He kept his eyes lowered.

"Then git about your work. We don' want no trouble." The hand gave him a hard shove.

Inside the mill Pete, the miller's helper, stared at Booker without speaking, though there were dancing lights in his eyes as if he wanted to laugh. The questions on Booker's lips died when he saw the forbidding face of the usually jovial sandy-haired miller.

When the corn was ground, Pete picked up the bags and carried them out. Standing in the doorway, Booker blinked his eyes in amazement as Pete strode by the white men. *Pete held his head high and brought his bare feet down hard on the ground!* The boy sucked in his breath with admiration. Then, after a moment's hesitation, he swallowed and followed after. For the life of him he couldn't keep *his* head up.

Pete tied the bags with quick, sure hands. "Up yo' go, small fry!" he said, and swung Booker onto the mare. Then the black face crinkled all over into a broad smile and Booker saw one of the sparkling eyes close in a conspiratorial wink!

By the time the boy could recover from his surprise the mare was well down the road. He did not look back. There were too many funny things going on. What did it mean? He pondered the question as they joggled along.

This was the first really nice day after a period of blustering winds and heavy rains. It was warm enough to shed the coarse flax shirt that scratched and bit into his flesh with every movement. Now the sun was warm on his bare back as he looked out over a fresh, clean world covered with quivering green. Life was very pleasant for the moment.

Suddenly the mare stepped into a hole and her small rider bounced into the air; something snapped and the wretched bags of corn dropped to the ground!

Booker surveyed the situation with more irritation than dismay. He was less than a mile from home and right at the crossroad coming out from Hale's Ford. Somebody would be along any minute.

"Yo' oughtta look where yo' goin'," he chided the mare, then sat down on the side of the road to wait.

But when he heard approaching footsteps he sprang up in alarm. Accompanying them were other sounds he did not like. He ran to the corner of the road. His fears were justified. They were soldiers! He looked around for a place to hide. This would mean the loss of his corn meal and Booker knew that supplies on the plantation were very low. All the frightful stories he had heard flashed through his head. But while he debated his course the soldiers were upon him.

"Lookee what's here!" called one.

Booker backed up against the mare, his eyes very round, his lips mute.

"He's scared stiff!"

"We're not going to hurt you, little fellow." The soldier who approached him loomed very big and his shaggy beard was formidable, but the voice was kind. "He's had an accident," he said when he saw the bags in the road. Turning back to the child, he asked, "Did your load fall off?"

Booker nodded.

One of the soldiers took up a bag and sniffed it. "Smells like corn," he told the others. "We could use this—"

"Leave it be, Jones!" ordered the big man, looking down at the little boy. "Live near here, boy?" When Booker nodded again the soldier said, "Well then, we'll just pick up this tyke's load and send him on his way."

Booker watched while two soldiers tied the bags to his horse. Then he looked up at the boss man and said, "Thankee, sah."

"Well, what do you know!" exclaimed a redheaded soldier with a young, freckled face. "It can talk. I thought the cat had your tongue, boy. Lemme see it!"

"Shut up, McGennis," snapped the big man. "Don't these people have enough to frighten them without your confounded teasing? Look at this kid's back!"

Booker lowered his eyes. He was sorry he had taken off his flax shirt. He was ashamed of those scars on his back. Nobody

25

said anything, but as he tried to pull up onto the horse the redheaded soldier picked him up and set him in place.

"Hurry home now," said the big man. "Tell your folks things are going to be better for them. The war's over. Lee has surrendered. You people are free—free to go wherever you wish—free to do what you like." He shook his head. "I guess you're too small to understand—but you tell them."

"Yessah! Yessah, I tell 'em," Booker promised.

The soldiers stood looking after the small boy on the big sagging horse. After a long moment the one called McGennis asked, "Now what can that poor black boy *do* with freedom?"

Late that night Booker's mother lay on her pallet and asked much the same question. In hundreds of cabins throughout the Southland black folks were asking, "What can I do with this freedom?"

The rags upon their backs belonged to somebody else. The roof over their heads, the pile of husks in the corner, the soil they had worked all their lives, the very hoe in their hand—all belonged to somebody else.

Jane rolled over onto her back and pondered. Where was Tom, her husband? Was he dead or alive? Would he come for her and the children? For the first time in months she was sleeping in the cabin. The Richmond relatives had gone in a flurry of haste and much talking. Jane thought of the high, strident voice sounding through the Big House that morning.

"It's foolhardy! That's what it is, foolhardy to stay way out here in this wilderness—miles from anybody. You'll be murdered in your beds!"

"Nonsense, Cousin Alice," Mistress Burroughs tried to soothe the woman. "Not one of our people would hurt a hair of our heads. This is our home. We'd be foolish to leave it."

"They murdered the West Indies planters. Being free will go to the blacks' heads! They're evil and vengeful! Well, I've warned you. We're going back to the city, where we'll have some protection. And I'm glad Anne's got sense enough to come along with us."

"I'm not going anywhere because I'm frightened, Aunt

Alice," Miss Anne spoke up with spirit. "I'm going to the city to see if there's anything I can do. Somebody's got to think about the future."

"Anne!"

The choked cry came from poor Missie. Jane did not have to see the tears in Mistress Burroughs eyes to understand. They had heard nothing from young Massa Chester. Poor Missie feared he was dead like Massa Billy. Miss Anne was all she had left. Now Miss Anne had gone away.

Jane turned her head and listened to the breathing of her three children. They were all in the cabin with her—John and Booker and small Mandy. Through a break in the thatched roof the mother could see a cluster of tiny stars. As she looked up, they twinkled in the darkness. She lifted her hand toward the stars, and the strength of her good right arm filled her with confidence.

"We'll make it," she said softly. "Now we're free!"

◆◆◆◆◆◆◆◆◆◆◆◆◆◆◆◆◆◆ **3** ◆◆◆◆◆◆◆◆◆◆◆◆◆◆◆◆◆◆

The Pilgrims

In the summertime a small boy grows like a weed and Booker was no exception. The lad swinging an ax at the edge of the woods this September morning was husky. His sturdy blows sent up a flock of squawking crows from the trees. Booker heard their frightened cries. He grinned and watched as they settled down in a distant meadow. Then he resumed his chopping.

As the sun climbed up the sky the day promised to be very warm. After a while Booker rested his ax and wondered if he and John might be able to get away for a swim. Six months ago such a thought would not have occurred to him but, since spring, conditions on the plantation had been very different.

Jones Burroughs, Esquire, master of the plantation, had called his former slaves together and told them they were free to go wherever they liked. He told them hands were still needed on the plantation, that any who wished could stay and work for him. The newly freed slaves listened in respectful silence. Not one of them would have harmed the master or any of his family. They felt sorry for them. What, many of them asked, would Old Marse and poor Missie do without their help? The old folks did not want to leave the only home they knew. Most of the young and strong had already gone.

Within a few days many of the cabins were deserted. Some set out to find long-lost relatives; some heard of a job in town and left. Husbands from other plantations arrived and took away their wives and children. The master was glad enough to devise plans for the future with those who were left. All were forced to consider the matter of providing food in a region where crops were devastated and cattle destroyed; where trading was wiped out and there was no money for whites or blacks. The nation as a whole wanted to forget the war and the slaves who were freed because of it.

While grownups struggled with these problems and the country mourned the tragic death of its President, black boys on the plantation got acquainted in ways other than in work gangs. With no lash likely to curl around bare shoulders they sat under spreading trees and talked, ran through the woods, and threw themselves into cooling streams. Fishing and hunting were encouraged by elders since meat was scarce. A broad catfish browned over a low fire furnished a meal for several hungry mouths, and a fat rabbit could be converted into a dish for company. Booker gained weight that summer.

This morning the boy had been sent to chop firewood. Now, with thoughts on swimming, he decided he had enough. The chunks piled in his arms were heavy and he staggered as he made his way around the field. When he reached the vegetable gardens behind the slave quarters, Booker sank down on a log to rest. Then he blinked his eyes rapidly and stared.

There in front of his cabin stood an ox cart! Even from this distance he could see that the cart was the center of attention. Folks were leaning out of doorways; children had gathered and were pointing at the ox. There was no sign of his mother. Evidently the driver of that cart was inside the cabin with her!

Forgetting his fatigue, Booker took up his wood and hurried toward the cabin as fast as his spindly legs would take him. John saw him coming and ran to meet him.

"From Pa!" the older boy exclaimed. "We got word from Pa. He sent for us! Come along, quick!"

John relieved his brother of most of the wood and together they hurried into the cabin. Booker saw his mother's shining face, then eyed the stranger who sat doubled up on the one bench in the cabin. He was so tall that he had to double up and his dark brown face was filled with shadows. Booker knew at once that he was a preacher. *He wore a coat, and shoes on his feet.*

"Hyear's my little boy, Booker, Brother Smith," said Jane at sight of the two boys. "Come 'long, Booker, speak nice to Brother Smith."

"Howdy, sah," murmured Booker.

"Fine family yo' got, Sistah," said the stranger. "Wall, I delivered Brother Tom's message. Now gotta be gettin' along on the Lawd's business."

"Oh, no!" exclaimed Jane in a shocked voice. "Yo' gotta eat! I wouldn't think o' lettin' you go without feedin' yo'."

No objection was offered and soon the whole quarter was involved in preparing a suitable meal for this man of God who traveled from place to place dispensing aid, comfort, and advice to a people suddenly faced with the responsibility of maintaining life under strange and hostile conditions.

Throughout the quarter excited tongues wagged. *Jane's husband was out West! He had a fine job! She was going to him!*

"Look what Pa sent!" John proudly held up a bundle of silky hides. "Beaver skins!" The ex-slaves gaped in wonder. That Tom must be rich! Nobody had ever seen such fine, soft skins.

Tom had also sent home a big sack of coarse salt. Brother Smith explained, "This salt come right from the salt mines.

Yo' can use hit anywhere for barter. Trade off these skins for to make yo' trip. They'll provide all yo' need."

John watered and fed the ox while Brother Smith ate in dignified silence. Then the Preacher rose to his full height and solemnly repeated instructions.

"Yo' all goin' to Malden, West Vi'ginnie." He took a stiff piece of paper out of his pocket and placed it in Jane's hands. "I writ down all the names of towns on the way. Show this paper and ask how to go. But yo' gotta 'member the name *Malden.*"

"Malden," repeated Jane, lifting her bright face. "Yes, yes, Brother Smith, I ain't gonna forget."

"An' make haste! Yo' must git ovah the mountains 'fore hit turn cold." He looked down at all of them and said, "God bless yo'! God keep the chillin safe!"

"Amen!" they responded. "Thankee, Brother Smith. God's will!"

Then the man of God was gone, doubled up in the little cart behind the big, slow-moving ox.

Within the next week Jane had to make many decisions. She would have consulted Missie, but the Big House was empty. Its owners had gone away for a while. If anybody was in charge it was Cripple Joe, and plans for traveling " 'way out West" were outside his experience.

It was finally agreed that the three biggest and thickest skins were fair payment for a two-wheeled cart, which stood unused in the stable, and a small one-eyed donkey. Everybody knew it would not be right to take either of the two mules, which were needed for plowing. Booker's old mare was considered, but there were well-founded doubts about her being equal to the trip. The one-eyed donkey was mangy but tough. Advice was plentiful as to what Jane should take: a skillet, certainly, for cooking on the roadside; some pieces of flint for striking up a fire; food. They had only the clothes on their backs. Granny Lou shook her head dolefully. She remembered when slaves received regular allowances of clothing.

" 'Tain't respectable," grumbled the old lady as she viewed

the rags Jane laid out in the sun to dry while her family remained indoors to hide their nakedness.

Granny Lou's stick went tapping around the yard as she hobbled from cabin to cabin. There was whispered consultation, several stealthy trips to the Big House, and gradually a more suitable wardrobe was assembled for the travelers.

Early on the morning of departure Booker donned a shirt which was far too big for him. But its smooth softness wrapped him in delight. For the first time in his life he stepped into pants. The legs had been cut, leaving a balloon-like fullness which in no way impeded the movements of Booker's legs, and he slipped quietly through the door. He had a little business of his own which demanded attention.

The cart stood packed and hitched. When Booker approached it a few minutes later, Cripple Joe was covering the back with a thick blanket formerly used for the saddle horses. There were no more saddle horses, so Cripple Joe thought the blanket might as well be used.

"What yo' got there, boy?" he asked, peering at Booker suspiciously.

After trying in vain to control the movements of something under his arm Booker threw back his shirt and revealed a small wiggling pig! It was the same weak little pig which Booker had tried to protect from the huge hogs. This pig had never reached its full size, thereby escaping the fate which befell its greedy fellows.

"Hit's my pig," said Booker with a touch of defiance. "I feed hit—I look after hit."

"Hum!" grunted the wizened little man. He thought a moment, then snatched the pig away from Booker, tossed a light rope about its body, tied the rope to the wagon, tucked the pig in the corner, and covered it with the blanket.

"Min' yo'," he said severely, *"Ah* didn't steal dat pig!"

Booker grinned and tucked his shirt well inside the billowing pants. Just in time, too, for now the whole quarter was turning out to see them off. Booker's eyes rounded at the sight of small Mandy, his sister. She had on a *white dress!* And John wore a jacket, but it didn't make him look like the Preacher.

31

Granny Lou showed her toothless gums in pride when Jane climbed up onto the cart. Missie might not have recognized her long-discarded dress, but the bonnet perched on Jane's head was the final badge of elevation from slavery to freedom!

"Good-bye! Good-bye!" They all waved their hands. They sounded happy. But Booker saw tears running down their cheeks. He looked around quickly as the cart began to move. *Where we goin'?* he wondered suddenly. He turned to his mother and saw that tears were also running down her cheeks.

They had nearly three hundred miles to go. Their route lay through a war-torn country, over rivers, between lofty peaks of the Alleghenies, across the Blue Ridge Mountains, and down into the valley of the Kanawha. Jane had been brought to Burroughs Plantation when she was a little girl and she had never left it. She did not know where she came from. She could not read the directions on the paper tucked in her bosom, but the name of her destination rang like a bell in her mind.

Malden! Malden, West Vi'ginnie!

The first day of travel was wonderful. They rode along an open road under a blue sky, passed fields and woods and houses, waved at people who stared after them. Finding their way to Roanoke was easy. This had been the big gay metropolis of the region. Jane had heard talk in the Big House about Roanoke. Miss Anne often went there for parties.

They did not stop until nightfall. Then they turned off beside a brook, where John first watered and fed the donkey. There was no need to cook anything this night. They ate heartily of food already prepared and packed for them. Afterward Jane spread the blanket on the ground and they lay down to rest.

As he lay staring up at the stars Booker resolved that henceforth he would always sleep in the open.

The second day they passed through Rocky Mountain, a drab, dusty little town which appeared to be almost deserted. They stopped at the market only long enough to ask a Negro standing on the corner for the road to Roanoke. A white man on horseback drew up his horse so that he could hear the inquiry. Seeing him, the Negro merely jerked his finger and pointed north.

They had some trouble that evening finding a good place to camp. The road was very bad. No trees lined the way; the meadows seemed furrowed up. Big holes gaped in the ground. There was a rancid, heavy smell in the air.

"Big fire!" exclaimed John, pointing to the charred ruins on the elevation.

The donkey pulled valiantly and the cart bumped over the desolate stretch. They did not know they were crossing a recent battlefield. But the next day they were far off their course, headed east.

So it was that they approached Roanoke on the main road coming from Richmond. After two days' wandering they were back on the route. Instead of following little-traveled back roads they were now on a main highway connecting two cities. Up and down the road moved a strange procession of carts, wagons, broken-down rigs, wheelbarrows, rusty baby carriages. The former slaves had set out to find freedom. With no place to go, they went everywhere—anywhere. The very old and very young rode in whatever there was to ride in. Others walked. The exodus was on. They had heard of a promised land. They were out to find it. All over the South ex-slaves were moving.

Broad fields rolled back from the highway, while beyond rows of hemlock and sycamore trees rose stately mansions. But now most of the mansions were empty. The fields once thick with ripening cotton or long, waving leaves of tobacco were covered with scrub and bush and short bluegrass. Black people who had toiled all day in these fields now stood idle at every crossing or joined the procession trudging in the dust beside the road.

"Eve'body goin' West, Ma?" asked John.

"I don' know, son. I don' know where the folks can go." Jane sighed with sympathy and thought how fortunate she and her children were. Tom had made a home for them in Malden. They had a good place to go.

Day was fading as they came to the Roanoke River and

33

could see the city on the other side. Jane had been anxious to get to Roanoke. Their food was running out. She would do some trading in the city. But now as she looked toward the sky she hesitated to cross the bridge. Townspeople would not like having their streets filled with stray wanderers. There might be trouble in the darkness. Best find a good stopping place for the night and enter Roanoke in the morning.

A few minutes later they were bumping over a side road. Jane headed for a cluster of trees on the edge of a field which suggested a quite spot for camping. When they drew near they saw that other travelers had had the same idea.

Three small children stood watching the cart approach. A young woman sat on a stump nursing an infant. An old woman and a man paused beside their pushcart.

"Howdy, folks!" Jane called out as she halted. They were in rags and revealed their heavy weariness as they responded in soft, polite voices.

"Let's eat, boys!" Jane's thought was to share what they had with this family. She would buy more food on the morrow.

Booker was first off the cart. His legs were cramped and he wanted to get his pig down on the ground. Only Mandy knew that the pig shared the cart with them. His mother and John took turns at driving and so rode on the front seat. Booker had managed to feed the pig surreptitiously and keep it hidden during the daytime.

"Wha' yo' from, daughtah?" The old woman hobbled forward, her bright eyes popping with curiosity.

"From down Hale's Ford way," answered Jane as she climbed over the wheel.

"Us from Richmond," announced the old woman proudly. "Us goin' tuh—" she was continuing when out of the shadows behind them came an angry bellow.

"Get off my land, ye black vermin! Get outta here!" A loud whistle and, "Here, boys, here! Drive these tramps off!" Hoarse barking surrounded them.

The woman with the baby sprang to her feet; the man tugged frantically at his precious cart, dragging it away from the bushes. The children ran toward the road. After a confused look around, Booker took out after them. For one moment

Jane stood paralyzed. Then she grabbed the young woman and pulled her toward the cart.

"Take me! Take me!" shrieked the old woman.

"Get the children!" yelled Jane.

Two ugly dogs crashed through the thicket and immediately set out after the fleeing children. The father grabbed a chunk of wood from the cart and ran into the road. John was pulling the women into the cart.

Jane saw one of the dogs spring; saw the little girl fall; saw the father stand over her trying to fight off the two snarling, leaping beasts!

"Don't ye touch my dogs, ye wretch!" shouted the master. He stopped at the edge of the trees and called, "Down, boys! Down!" The dogs backed away but continued slowly circling the man and the little girl on the ground. The red-faced man in a leather jacket regarded the terrified group with cold contempt. "Now get your young'uns away from here. This will teach you to stay away from these parts. Here, dogs!"

He stood with his dogs and watched while they carried the little girl to the cart. Her shoulder was torn and blood dripped down into the dust. Nobody said a word, though the young mother and small Mandy were crying softly.

Booker and the two other children stopped some distance down the road and looked back. They could dimly see the rest coming toward them and they waited. The father picked up the smallest child and set her in his hand cart. Booker and a boy about his own size walked close beside the man. The donkey cart was full.

Jane had no idea where this road would take them. Nobody inquired. They were all too glad just to get away. The river ran to the north. At the first crossing Jane turned in that direction. This was a wooded lane and soon darkness shut them in.

"Yo' scared?" Booker asked the boy at his side.

"Naw," came the reply.

Booker clamped his teeth tight and stumbled along. He could think of many places he would rather be than in the woods at night.

Darkness did not seem to bother the donkey. The cart

35

bumped along without mishap until gradually the trees thinned, they came out into the open, and Jane said triumphantly, "Dar's the river!"

They all leaned forward thankfully. Some deep, ancient urge drew them to the water. From the rivers came life. Rivers often meant safety to the slaves. Now these sore and weary freedmen knew that they could lie down by the river and rest. As they moved slowly down toward the bank they caught the flare of fires around the bend; they heard voices calling out. Booker sniffed the air and grinned.

"Hurry!" he urged the other boy. "We gotta eat."

In a few minutes they came up to other campers on the river's edge. No need now to rub the flint for a light. Willing hands started their fire and experienced nurses tended the injured child.

The fires died down. The dust and dirt of the road disappeared; the anxious faces softened. Here and there low, throaty laughter sounded in the night. Moonlight lay on the river, touched the top of the trees, and here and there became a silver shaft of magic. Suddenly music sounded. Somebody plucked a banjo and filled the night with a gay, rollicking tune. Then a strong, happy voice burst into song:

> "Walk togethah, chillin,
>   Don't yo' get weary—
> Walk togethah, chillin,
>   Don't yo' get weary—
> Walk togethah, chillin,
>   Nevah get weary—
> Dar's a Great Camp Meetin'
>   In da Promised Land."

Before the chorus was finished people were swaying in unison. When the voice repeated the first phrase, men, women, and children were ready with the response:

> "Don't yo' get weary!"

36

With one voice they shouted:

> "Dar's a Great Camp Meetin'
> In da Promised Land."

The chorus sank to a hum when a harmonious chord sounded on the banjo. Then the first voice rose in an ecstasy of joy:

> "Gonna sing an' nevah ti-yah,
> Sing an' ne-vah ti-yah-ah-ah,
> Sing an' nevah ti-yah-ah-ah-ah . . ."

It was a golden lute tossing a promise to the stars. Deep in every heart they made the pledge—never, never to turn back! Always, always to press forward—always to find a song in their hearts. The strong young voice led them on until once more the ex-slaves sang together:

> "Dar's a Great Camp Meetin'
> In da Promised Land."

A week more brought Booker and his family well up into the Allegheny foothills. Traveling was now harder. Roads were steep and rocky. They saw few dark faces. The small farmers of this region had held few slaves. Those few had either gone away or had found work in the community.

A storm caught the travelers some miles west of Clifton Forge. They could find no place to take shelter and were frightfully lashed by winds and rain. But the following evening a Dutch farmer took them in. His wife gave them hot food. They were able to dry their clothes and sleep in the barn. The farmer shook his head in dismay when Booker's mother said they were going on over the mountains.

"You cannot make it in a donkey cart!" he exclaimed. He measured distance with his hands. "Too high! Too steep!"

But Jane pushed on.

They had never seen mountains. John's face grew taut and still as the cart edged around sharp corners, as they skidded along narrow ledges. Booker did not know the many dangers he escaped. He remembered his cramped limbs. He remembered the cold at night. He rememberd bitterly that they ran out of food. The one terrible thing about the whole trip was that he had lost his pig!

Jane scolded Booker when she discovered the small pig. But the day they sat huddled together in a mountain cave she knew that if they did not reach a settlement soon they would have to eat Booker's pig. The flurry of snow continued throughout the night. The next morning they could not find the pass. For two days they wandered lost in the mountains. At the end of the second day John took the little pig some distance away and killed it.

Booker ate nothing until they arrived at the town.

Somehow they got through. The day came when they dropped down into the valley of the Great Kanawha River—into a world clothed in lovely fall colors: warm brown, red, yellow, and rusty green. Their eyes were heavy for lack of sleep, but now sleep seemed unnecessary. That night long after sundown they saw a glow in the sky ahead. They pushed on along a road which was no longer dark, turned a bend, and looked down upon what looked like a lake of fire! They could see nothing burning, and yet flames licked into the air out of swirling eddies which might have been liquid gold!

John gasped, "Ma! Hit's lak the mouth o' Hell!"

Afterward they learned that they had passed Burning Springs, a natural phenomenon caused by gas escaping through the ground.

They were a sorry sight limping into Malden. One wheel was broken and the donkey was lame. Their fine clothes were torn, dirty, and stained.

But joy shone from Jane's haggard face when the first coal-blackened miner she called to answered, "Sure thing, sister, this hyear's Malden!"

The woman lifted her hands high and said, "Thank God! Thankee, Jesus!"

4

What's in a Name?

Booker strode along briskly trying to keep pace with the
tall man beside him. It was still dark and the chill in the air
bit through his jeans. He hunched his shoulders and set his
teeth more firmly while his bright eyes darted about with
interest. He had a job! He was going to earn wages! He
watched shadowy figures emerge from huts, saw them join
groups going the same way, and heard greetings. He thought
how nice it would be if somebody hailed him. One month after
his arrival in Malden, Booker was on his way to the saltworks
near Washington's Plot.

Long before the advent of white men Indians knew that
great buffaloes came to these marshes to lick salt. The first
white settlers called the place Buffalo Lick. After the buffaloes
were killed or driven away the settlers scooped up the briny
water and secured salt for their own uses. Later came specula-
tors and businessmen who started a lucrative salt industry.
Among the early surveyors of the area was a young Virginian
named George Washington. The town which sprang up near
the salt marshes cherished this memory and proudly called a
section after the Father of their Country. The Civil War had
wiped out Malden's extensive industry. Now, with the war
over, salt makers were attempting to resume operation. They
brought in the cheapest possible labor and operated the old
furnaces with the least expense. Rather than undertake costly
repairs they revived discarded old methods of securing salt.
Laborers were plentiful. And to ex-slaves any wages seemed
wonderful. Tom was only one of many men who were glad to
get a job under any condition.

39

Almost Jane's first thought at the sight of her husband was that she would have to "feed 'im up." She shook her head and murmured, "Yo' sure needs woman to cook good victuals."

Tom's gaunt face twisted into a smile. At last he had his family! Though he was not the father of Jane's two boys, he welcomed John and Booker as heartily as he did his own little Mandy. Jane saw this and warm gratitude filled her heart. She looked at her girl child and thanked God her daughter would never know what slavery meant to dark women. Mandy was free!

The shack Tom had ready for them was little better than the plantation cabin. It was the only place he could rent, however, and Jane was happy. She swept and cleaned and scrubbed. She sent the boys out for long reeds which she spliced together and used to divide the shack into two rooms. Only one thing worried her: there was no garden.

"Where we plant 'taters?" she asked anxiously.

"Can't plant nothin', honey," Tom told her. "We gets all we needs from da sto'e."

"Get 'taters from sto'e, and co'n an' beans?" asked Jane in amazement.

"Eve'ythin'," Tom assured her.

Jane turned away with some misgivings. Food, she reasoned, should be grown in the ground.

Tom's wages amounted to about fifty cents a day. This was not paid in money but in company script, which was accepted at the company store in payment for the workers' supplies.

After several visits to the store Jane could not understand why there was not enough script to buy the food they needed.

"Yo' gotta learn how to buy!" stormed Tom, who was giving her everything he earned. "Yo' gits too much!"

"But we gotta eat!" wailed Jane. "Iffen we had a garden Ah could—"

"Stop talkin' 'bout gardens!" Tom cut her off impatiently. "We ain't no plantation hands! Ah earns wages!" His face suddenly brightened. "Ah bet Ah find jobs fur the boys! Dey's big an' strong!"

But John was not so strong. Jane was worried about his

40

cough and shortness of breath. So it was Booker who hurried along through the November morning clutching the lunch his mother had fixed for him.

The sun was not yet up when they reached the saltworks. Tom hurried Booker along to the building where hiring was done. Early as it was, groups of idle workers stood about hopefully waiting to be called. Booker felt uncomfortable as he and his father immediately went inside. The place was like a heated oven.

"Hyear's mah boy, boss, suh," Tom said, pushing him forward. The sudden blast of a whistle drowned out anything further. Tom hustled away, leaving Booker standing alone.

"Right over there," ordered the red-faced man behind a table. Booker quickly joined a group of white and black boys standing against the wall. They were all equally gaunt, ragged, and dirty.

The larger boys stared hard and one of them muttered, "Jus' outta da cotton patch!"

The snickers died as the boss came up with a sharp "Come along!"

Booker fell into step with the others and followed. After the intolerable heat of the low shed with its brick furnaces, the outdoor chill struck him like a knife. Gray mist rolled over the treeless barrens where here and there long sheds such as the one they had left belched smoke into a gray sky. Here Campbell Creek spread out into a dozen pools or pockets. Some of the pools were natural; others were the result of wells dug in the search for salt.

In a few minutes the boys reached one of these pools and halted. Booker looked about with interest, quickly noting the big round cylinders, ropes, shovels, buckets, and casks which lined the edge of the water. Then he saw the big holes in the ground, and the men who suddenly appeared with great hooks and grapples. The boss yelled something. The men seized one of the cylinders with their hooks and lowered it into a hole. The boss yelled again and, while Booker stared with his mouth open, two of the boys hopped into the same hole!

"Let her go!" called the boss.

41

With much straining, with shouts and curses, the men let out the ropes and for what seemed to Booker an interminable length of time the cylinder went down into the earth.

The next minutes added to Booker's confusion. As one boy after another disappeared into the holes he tried in vain to figure out what was happening. Evidently he would have to go into a hole. But why? Nobody had told him anything about his work. What was he to do? Where was he going? He looked around wildly, but nobody paid any attention to him.

At last only he and one other boy were left. This time, when the boss yelled, the other boy turned his head and said, "Dat's us! Let's go, bo'!"

Grateful for this gesture of comradeship, Booker clutched his lunch tighter and started after the larger boy.

"Hey, new boy! Whatchu carryin'? Drop it!" The boss had finally noticed Booker.

He looked about nervously, then laid his lunch on an overturned cask near the hole.

"Awright," growled the red-faced foreman, "climb in! Hold the rope!"

The other boy had already disappeared into the ground. Booker seized the rope and cautiously lowered himself.

"Find da bar wid yo' foot, bo'!" came up from the darkness below him.

Holding the rope tightly, Booker felt about with one foot until he encountered a crosspiece. But he had hardly braced himself when everything seemed to fall away into a blast of sound. For awful moments he dropped through space while nauseous waves shook him. Then a hard, grinding thump loosened his hold on the rope, water dashed over him, and he fell to the bottom of the well!

"Yo' awright, kid?"

Booker gasped and sputtered. The water was shallow, but it was icy cold. He tried to get up, but everything he touched was slippery. The clammy darkness choked him. Then firm hands dragged him to his feet. He leaned against the dripping wall and panted for breath.

"Dar yo' be!" encouraged the other boy. "Watch out—hyear come da buckets!"

Booker looked up and saw something descending upon them from the faint circle of light far above their heads. He controlled his shaking jaws enough to ask, "What we gonna do?"

"Fill des hyear buckets," announced the boy with cheerful assurance. "Hyear's yo' shovel." Booker's stiff fingers closed about a handle put in his hands. His eyes had adjusted themselves to the gloom. He could see the larger boy attach the buckets to hooks in the wall, could almost see the grin on his face as he picked up another shovel and said, "Now, kid, dig! Jus' dig and put eve'yt'ing yo' dig in des buckets." And the boy sank his shovel into the shifting mud at his feet.

Booker followed suit. The space in which they worked was too small for free movements, but within a short time Booker found that by bracing his feet in the water and twisting his body he could get his shovel to the bucket. The exertion made his blood race and drove the chill out of his body. In a little while he was aching all over. But after a time, as one bucket after another was sent up, he no longer ached. He no longer felt anything.

How long he stayed in the salt well that first day Booker did not know. When the signal came and they were drawn up in the hollow drum, he collapsed on the ground. When he sat up and looked about for his lunch he could not find it.

The foreman did not send the new boy down into the well again that day. Instead Booker was set to cleaning the casks which were to receive the refined salt.

At the end of the day the boss came up to Booker and said, "You'll do, boy. Here's your number. Come back tomorrow."

Booker took the clean yellow square handed him. His hands were grimy and he hated to dirty anything so fine. He searched in vain for a clean place to put the card, for now he was as filthy as any of the boys he had seen that morning. Yet, now, nobody looked at him with hostility; nobody snickered as he crossed the yard. Now he belonged. He was earning wages!

At home Booker showed the card proudly. "See mah number!"

His mother held the square close to the tallow light and

turned it wistfully from side to side. She wished she could read it.

"Dat's fine!" she told her son, though her eyes were not happy as she looked down at the bruised, dirty little fellow whom she had sent away freshly washed that morning.

While he hungrily ate beans and corn pone Booker described the saltworks to his brother. John's coughing interrupted the story at intervals, but he listened eagerly.

"Ah'll be goin' out next week," promised the older boy.

"Sho! Sho!" assented Booker. He had not mentioned his hardships.

When Tom came in later he also was shown the card. "Yo' gotta learn yo' number," he told Booker.

"Learn hit?"

"Yep." Tom took an old, tattered card from his pocket. "Look hyear! Ah knows dat number wherever Ah sees hit."

Booker gazed hard at the smudged, wrinkled surface. He held his own smooth, fresh card beside Tom's and a broad grin spread over his face.

"Mah number's lak Pa's!" he exclaimed.

"Sho' 'nough," Tom agreed. "Well, now, dat number's *eighteen.*"

Jane's eyes shone as she looked from one to the other.

Tom clapped his hand on Booker's shoulder and cautioned, "Remember dat, boy! Yo' gotta know dat sign when yo' sees hit!"

"Yo' gonna learn to read!" exclaimed the mother. Her eyes beamed with pride.

Booker learned the "sign" and thus mastered his first reading lesson. Within a short time he not only knew that his number was eighteen but could scratch out the number on his buckets and salt casks. The foreman noticed that here was a bright boy. When the works shut down that winter for two months, Booker was told to report back for work in the spring.

Meanwhile Jane had found a way to earn "wages." There were only two or three fine homes on the outskirts of Malden where servants were regularly employed. But among the moderately well off it was the custom to hire a weekly washwoman and an occasional cleaning woman. The pay was poor, but Jane was willing and able. Housewives were glad to get her.

One day when Jane was cleaning out a clothes closet the lady of the house said, "And throw out those old schoolbooks. Ned finished with them long ago. They're just cluttering up his room. Throw them away!"

Jane looked down at the books scattered on the floor with old shoes, caps, ice skates, and boots—and her heart leaped. Schoolbooks! She knew that it was a crime for a slave to have a book. But she was free! Dare she tell the lady she would like to have them? She thought about Booker's painful efforts with his number. She stooped and picked up one of the books.

"Don't dawdle—er— What did you say your name is? Oh, yes, Jane. Well, hurry, Jane! Do finish upstairs before the children get home from school!"

Without a word Jane gathered up the books and carried them downstairs. *They'll be burned,* she thought despairingly. She carried them out to the shed and let them fall into the trash bin. Then she hurried back to the house.

For the rest of the day while she swept and scrubbed and cleaned and polished Booker's mother thought of the books lying out there in the bin. It was dark by the time she finished work and left by the back door. So no one saw her slip into the shed, stoop quickly, tuck something under her shawl, and hurry away into the winter evening.

Jane was breathless when she reached home, but her triumphant announcement could be heard in the next shack, "Ah gotta book fur yo'!"

Booker turned the frayed pages of the old Webster's "blueback" speller eagerly. Here were all the letters! Now he could learn all "the readin'."

Soon the whole community of crowded shacks hummed with excitement. Ex-slaves were no longer afraid to talk about a book or to express their burning desire to read. Poor white neighbors laughed at such nonsense. What could blacks do with "learnin' "!

With the combined help of two or three neighbors who

45

recognized some of the letters, Booker learned the alphabet. He pored over meaningless syllables such as *ab, ba, ca,* and *da.* He tried to memorize each page! Folks began noticing him. Old people nodded with approval when the boy passed. They mumbled, "Dat boy's gotta head on shouldah!"

In the spring Booker took his brother, John, down into the salt wells with him. The younger boy was a good teacher and the foreman noticed that the two together did an excellent job. Soon Booker was marking not only his own casks but others. And he was slowly spelling out words.

That summer Tom went to work in a coal mine some distance away from Malden. His day was longer because he had to travel several miles each morning in the company truck and the mine whistle blew at six o'clock. But his pay was better.

Freedom's good, thought the mother as she hung her washing in the cubicle of space behind the shack. Close by, a baby cried lustily; a dog sniffed near her feet and had to be shooed away; coarse voices rose in dispute. There was the clatter of pots and pans, the rub-dub of a washboard; children were calling out and a woman was singing.

"Mawnin', sistah," called a neighbor.

"Mawnin' to yo'self," answered Jane. "Hit's a fine mawnin', ain't hit?"

"Deed 'tis, sistah; deed 'tis."

They worked as hard as they had in slavery, but now each week, each month was a victory won. When winter came again, the shack was reenforced against snowdrifts and icy winds. The charcoal burner gave out a cheerful glow and Booker knew he would always find a bowl of something hot and filling when he reached home at night. Small Mandy was not strong enough to lift the heavy iron kettle, but she could fill and wash the bowls. In fact, with Jane also working away from home most of the day, Mandy was doing most of the cooking, sweeping, and tending of fires. Mandy was getting to be a "big girl." Jane smiled happily every time she looked at Mandy. At times, however, when Booker's wide eyes looked up at his mother her heart twisted. The boy was too thin. The slight body was not sufficient to support his big head. He

46

scarcely ever had time any more to "read" his book.

Then a teacher came to Malden!

Ben Coleman came to Malden from Marietta, Ohio, searching for relatives of his father. Years before, the elder Coleman had escaped from slavery; subsequently he bought free papers and settled in Ohio, where he ran a blacksmith shop. He had tried in vain to secure the freedom of other members of his family. When the war was over he dared go back to Georgia and look for them. They were all gone. Where? Father and son went from place to place following every clue. In time one clue led to Malden, West Virginia, and so young Ben Coleman came and went from shack to shack asking questions.

Black folks and white gazed with awe-stricken eyes upon this clean young Negro who *wrote down in a book* while they answered him. They pointed to a newspaper sticking out of his pocket. Children cautiously touched his polished boots.

"He talk lak gentry! He walk lak gentry!" they whispered. Then ex-slaves looked at one another, their faces beaming as they added, "An' he black!"

Everybody in the shacks tried to be helpful, but Ben Coleman found no trace of relatives. The young man crossed to the other side of town and came to another neighborhood where Negroes lived. These were "old settlers." Some had lived in West Virginia for years as free Negroes—carpenters, bricklayers, a wheelwright. Others had been favored slaves in Big Houses of the region and now worked for wages in the homes of mine owners or salt makers. Here the houses were neat, with porches and curtained windows. Here was an African Methodist Episcopal Church and a Reverend Johnson who alternated Sunday preaching between Malden and Parkersville, a town fifty miles northwest. Fortunately Ben Coleman found Reverend Johnson at home. The pastor listened sympathetically but could offer little by way of encouragement.

"It's so hard for the freedman to find work that he goes from place to place. No one knows where he goes or how he exists. He has no name, no address. He cannot read a letter, though it be delivered to him!" Reverend Johnson shook his head. "I doubt if your father finds his people."

Ben Coleman frowned. "I couldn't help feeling that any or all of those poor wretches in those miserable huts were my relatives. The filth about those cabins is intolerable!"

"The decent people of Malden are ashamed of that section. It's a motley mixture of the poorest, most ignorant and degraded whites with bewildered, awkward plantation hands just out of slavery. Drinking, gambling, and fighting are frequent. I've tried to get them to come to church, but they won't. It's terrible for the children."

"They need a school," murmured the young man.

"A school!" exclaimed the Preacher. "That's what every Negro around here is talking about. We must have a school. I have a Sunday school here in the church, but instead of Bible lessons I'm teaching parents and children to read!"

Ben Coleman smiled. "They'd like that story at Oberlin, sir."

"You've been to Oberlin!" exclaimed the Preacher. "You studied at Oberlin College?"

"Yes, sir," responded the young man modestly. "Some of the students there are going South to teach with the Freedmen's Bureau. I'm thinking of joining them."

"Then you're a *teacher*!"

Reverend Johnson seized the young man's hand. He urged him to stay and meet other Negroes in the community. They would work out plans to hire a teacher.

"Negroes here need a teacher as badly as in any part of the South," declared Reverend Johnson. "Come to Malden!"

Ben Coleman returned home to Marietta with this admonition ringing in his ears. Every Negro who could get to him had added his plea. He had the assurance that each family would pay a certain amount each month, that he would be given board and room in the various homes of his pupils, that his school could be housed in the church. Two weeks later he wrote Reverend Johnson that he would come.

A school for Negroes was something new and unheard of—another wonderful manifestation of freedom! There were no free public schools in Malden. Those who could afford it sent their youths and, far less frequently, their young ladies away to school. Poor white children did not go to school at all. White people, therefore, heard with some amazement that Negroes were going to have a "pay school."

Jane heard about the school and immediately began pondering how she could send her boys—especially Booker. This would take money and the boys would have to give up their jobs at the saltworks! Jane frowned and set her teeth. They must have "learnin' "! There had to be a way.

Booker passed along the exciting news to John. "A school, boy! Readin' an' writin' an' figgerin'! Ah could learn eve'ything!"

John shrugged his shoulders. "We gotta work," he said wearily. "We ain't goin' no place eve'y day but to Washington's Plots."

"Ah'm askin' Ma," Booker declared stoutly.

His mother knew what was on his mind when her youngest son impatiently pushed aside his bowl that night.

"Ma, gonna be a school!" he blurted out.

She turned away miserably, dreading what she would have to say.

"Ah wanna go!"

"Yo' Pa say—" she began, then changed to, "We ain't got the price, son."

"But, Ma, Ah could—" Booker's words died at the look on her face.

Booker heard his brother's snort of disgust. He ate nothing more.

Later that night Tom was more specific. He told Booker, "Us poor folks gotta work to get ahead. School kin wait."

Booker did not notice the coming of spring as he trudged to and from work in the days which followed. His unhappy face wrung his mother's heart. She managed to add a pittance to her own meager earnings. But when she offered it as an argument in Booker's behalf her husband growled, "The boy's doin' good. Leave 'im be!"

The school opened in May and Ben Coleman did not lack pupils. The teacher was somewhat appalled by the numbers of old folks who hobbled to the church. Being too old to work, they joyfully seized this opportunity to read the Bible before they died! Mothers came with children who could scarcely walk, some with infants in their arms. It seemed that few were too young, and none too old, to make the attempt to learn.

One afternoon shortly after the opening, Coleman finished picking up after his turbulent classes, rearranged the chairs, and with a sigh of relief closed the church door behind him. As he turned to leave he was confronted by a tall, raw-boned dark woman who had evidently been waiting for him. She stood firmly on bare feet; her head was covered with a coarse cloth. Coleman at once saw her intelligent eyes and the determined set of her square chin.

"Mistah Teachah," she said softly, "Ah wanna speak wid yo'."

"Yes, ma'am," the young man responded gravely. "What did you want to say?"

The woman swallowed. She drew in a deep breath, as a swimmer does before diving into the water. Then her words came in a rush.

"Mah boy wanna go tuh school. His Pa say he gotta work. Mah boy sma't; he know readin'. He gotta book. Mah boy wanna learn."

Ben Coleman understood. He looked away. What could he tell this anxious mother? All the longing of a newly emancipated people sounded in her voice. The teacher was already struggling with many unexpected problems. What could he do in a case like this? The woman was plucking at his sleeve.

"We kin pay. We got money. See!" her soft voice insisted.

She held out her hand and he saw the silver pieces lying on her worn palm. He saw the scars and calluses on the fingers and he asked, "Does your boy work all day every day?"

"Eve'y day 'cept Sunday," she answered quickly. "Ah thought maybe—on Sunday—yo' might—" Her courage failed and she whispered, "We kin pay. Take hit!"

Ben Coleman sighed and gently pushed her open hand away.

"First I must talk to your boy, ma'am. Tell him to come and see me Sunday morning—not too early." He pointed to a cottage across the way. "I live right there with Mr. Jones, the wheelwright. Tell him to bring his book."

Her face was beaming now. "Yessah, yessah, Mistah Teachah!"

"What's his name?"

"Booker."

"Booker—"

"Yessah, jus' Booker."

She hurried away then, leaning slightly forward, as if her legs could not carry her quickly enough. He knew she was used to walking over fields and that she had carried many heavy loads. He remembered that slaves had no surnames. Many of the ex-slaves had already acquired last names; some took the names of former masters. A surname was a free Negro's badge of honor. Booker, thought Ben Coleman, was an odd name for a boy.

Jane, too, was thinking about names. She said nothing to Tom about her visit to the teacher, but she did say, "Tom, we gotta have a name!"

"Eh, what?" asked Tom. Every bone in his body ached with fatigue.

"A name. 'Tain't right us be jus' Tom an' Jane lak when we slaves. We free now. We gotta have a family name!"

"Hum-hum," grunted Tom, and sank under waves of sleep.

Nothing troubled Booker the next Sunday morning. The teacher had said "not too early," so he waited impatiently until the sun was well up in the sky. Then, taking his book, he fairly ran the distance across town.

Ben Coleman smiled at the boy's striking resemblance to his mother. He was lighter in color, but his level glance was like hers; the set of his small chin was like hers, and the way he thrust forward his head. Coleman did not ask Booker's age because he knew that children born in slavery had no birthdays—no exact date was recorded—but he judged the boy to be twelve or thirteen years old.

"All right, Booker," the young man said genially, "let's read!"

So Booker's schooling began—for, hereafter, every Sunday

morning he "went to school." Ben Coleman furnished him with a simple reader, a slate, and a slate pencil. The boy learned rapidly. Now, in summer, he had a little daylight each evening for study. He would eat only after it was too dark to read.

Ben Coleman closed his school the end of July after announcing that it would reopen the middle of September. He told Booker, "When I come back I'm going to see your father. You ought to be in a class. You're my best pupil and I want to show you off!"

August stretched interminably. About the middle of the month Booker was taken out of the salt wells and given more important work in the store and shipping rooms, with a slight increase in pay. His ability to read and write a little was already proving to be an asset. He felt important as he went from one cask to another chalking numbers on them. He read the labels on incoming goods and stored the stock accordingly. As September approached, the boy looked out across the marshes called Washington's Plots and fixed his determination. *He would go to school.*

On the first day of September, Booker told his foreman that he could work only half a day.

"What's wrong with you, for Pete's sake?"

"I wanna go to school."

The foreman gasped. But like everybody else in Malden he had heard of the Negro school. He was annoyed because he needed the boy. As he told the boss later, "The little rascal's bright. Says he'll come in an hour earlier and return in the evenings."

"Half a day!" growled the boss. "Get somebody else."

The foreman scratched his head. "I need him, boss," he said slowly.

"Aw, then don't bother me," snapped the boss. "Work it out your own way!"

It was finally settled that Booker would work from six until nine every morning and from three until six every afternoon. He would be paid for half a day.

At home Tom roared with rage. But Jane stoutly backed up her son. Tom saw that there was no use opposing her.

52

"Whar yo' all gonna get the money?" he asked mockingly.

"Ah got hit," said Jane quietly.

On the opening day of school Booker sat well up toward the front of the church. Ben Coleman saw him immediately and smiled with pleasure. Other new faces eagerly looked up at the teacher. Some of the former pupils were missing. But the little church was packed with the same expectancy and high hopes as before. The teacher squared his shoulders.

"I am happy to be back with you again." Shuffling feet expressed their shy joy and Coleman continued. "We're going to work harder than ever and we'll move forward rapidly. First let's get the names." As he drew a large sheet of paper toward him he directed his smile in Booker's direction. "I recognize one new pupil and I'm very glad to see him." They followed the teacher's glance to the boy in coarse jeans who was twisting his bare feet in obvious embarrassment. "I don't have to ask his name. I know it's Booker."

He bent his head to write but was interrupted by a loud "Booker? Booker what?"

The boy who asked the question twisted around and stared disdainfully at the new pupil. Booker did not lower his eyes. He recognized the stare for what it was. This boy, only slightly bigger than he, was of the favored group who lived in neat cottages. No doubt his people had been free a long time. He had a *family* name. And now he would taunt a "stupid plantation hand" who had no last name! Even while Booker's nimble brain was taking this in, another part of his mind was meeting the challenge. Out of the well of his thoughts one name came instantly. He stood up and lifted his head.

"Mah las' name's Washington, sah. Mah name's Booker Washington." He shot a triumphant look at the other boy and sat down.

Ben Coleman hid his smile and gravely wrote the name at the top of his sheet. He suspected his pupil's invention, but he admired the boy's selection. For, though he had merely taken the name of the salt marshes where he worked, Booker had unwittingly named himself after George Washington, Father of his Country.

Out of the Mines

Up and out before dawn! Two miles to work . . . roll casks in place . . . drag sacks, check lumber, go here, go there! Hurry! Nine o'clock, and away through the woods, down side streets, across back yards to school! *Please recite, Booker! Read . . . write . . . Three times three is nine . . . What time is it, sir?* Time to go back to work. *Here, boy, mark these casks! You're late—now hurry!*

School started at nine and Booker keenly felt the inconvenience of always arriving late. Years afterward the famous educator told in his *Up from Slavery* of a device which, for a time, enabled him to reach school by nine o'clock:

> There was a large clock in the little office of the salt-works. All the hundred or more workmen depended upon this clock to regulate their hours of beginning and ending the day's work. Morning after morning I managed to slip into the office and without being seen I moved the clock hands from half-past eight up to the nine o'clock mark. In time the boss discovered that something was wrong and locked the clock case. I did not mean to inconvenience anybody. I simply meant to reach school on time.

That winter Booker hurried through hard, driving rain, blustery winds, snowstorms, and silent cold. The problem of clothing her younger son taxed Jane's abundant resourcefulness. Had it not been for the castoffs given her in the homes where she now daily found work, Jane could not have coped with the situation. For Booker was growing rapidly in body as well as in mind.

Then disaster struck. The saltworks closed abruptly, with gloomy rumors that the owners were abandoning the furnaces. Three days later Tom fell in the mine and broke his leg.

There was no miners' insurance in those days. An accident was an "act of God" deplored by the company but for which it accepted little responsibility. The company doctor called and set Tom's leg. That was all. The injured miner was off "without pay."

Gloom settled within the shack where the sick man groaned and tossed. Mandy did what she could during her mother's long absences. Booker went off to school unhappily and returned to face reproach. He called his brother, John, outside and the two whispered together.

"Railroad's buildin' track out to the mine," John told him. "Bet we could git work out dar." He paused for Booker's comment. When none came, the older boy added, "Pa say dey'd take us on at the mine."

Booker shuddered. Nearly every day somebody got hurt in the mines. Everybody talked about the accidents, but men and boys continued to go out there to work. Moreover, thought Booker dismally, miners were dirty all the time. No amount of scrubbing removed the coal grime from their bodies and clothes. Yet something had to be done. As things were, only their mother was earning wages.

"Let's try the railroad," suggested Booker.

"Suits me," agreed John, and off they went.

The track boss glanced at them briefly and saw that they lacked the strength necessary to swing the huge hammers used for driving pile. He shook his head.

The mine boss was not so discriminating. In fact, thin boys could crawl through tunnels too small to admit a man. This was often advantageous in a mine when new pits were opened. John and Booker were told to report the next morning at six o'clock.

When his favorite pupil missed school for two consecutive days, Ben Coleman came inquiring for him. Mandy stood in the doorway of the shack and shook her head.

"He ain't hyear," she said, while her eyes scrutinized the stranger.

"Is your Ma home, little girl?" Coleman knew this must be Booker's sister. "I'd like to see her."

"Nossah."

"Who dar, Mandy?" called a hoarse voice from the dim interior.

"It's the teacher." Coleman peered over Mandy's head. "I'm asking about Booker. He wasn't at school."

His announcement brought a groan, a curse, a growl. "He workin'." Another groan, and then an irritable "Go 'way! Leave us alone!"

"Pa sick," Mandy explained softly, "awful sick."

The young man looked down at the child. He felt sick himself. "I'm sorry, Mandy," he whispered. "When will your Ma be home?"

The grave little face beamed with smiles. "Yo' knows mah name!" She took a step forward. "Ma coming'—"

"Mandy!" The harsh shout shook them. "Shut dat do'!"

Her frightened look implored forgiveness before she slammed the door in his face. Ben Coleman turned away helplessly. He understood all too well. What could he do? *These people need help!* In his distress he went to the Preacher.

"One after another the boys drop out," Coleman told him. "I know they have to work. But how can the race advance if only the aged and infirm attend school? His shoulders slumped. "This boy, Booker, was the brightest of them all. Can't we do something?" he asked urgently.

"I can at least call on the sick man," Reverend Johnson said patiently, "and try to give some friendly assistance to the boy's mother."

"She won't accept charity. I know she won't take charity!" There was bitter resignation in the young man's voice. "They'll all work themselves to death, but they won't take charity."

"Don't be discouraged, my young friend. God's ways are not our ways. He has brought our people out to freedom. He will not desert us now." After a moment of silence he asked,

"What's the name of this family?"

"Washington," answered Coleman. "The boy's name is Booker Washington." He sighed. "Say that I'll gladly teach Booker on Sundays as I did last summer."

Reverend Johnson hastened to keep his word. He prayed beside the injured man's cot and delivered the teacher's message. The following Sunday afternoon his wife, with two other women, visited "Sistah Washin'ton." They brought food, ostensibly for the sick husband, and several pieces of clothing for the little girl. Jane received them politely and promised to attend church as soon as her husband was on his feet again.

Booker did not respond to his teacher's invitation. With the sunlight gone from his life the boy no longer hoped or dreamed. He longed only for the moment when he came up out of the ground, when he could breathe. Work in the coal mine was not only hard and dangerous but dulling and brutalizing. Booker burrowed through the earth like an animal, not upright as men walk, but bent and doubled to his knees, frequently almost prone on the ground. Miners were driven exactly as the donkeys were driven, harshly, merciless, unceasingly. It was easy to get lost in the labyrinth of black pits. Sometimes the boy's tiny light would go out; then he would crawl about in the blackest darkness—a darkness which often resounded with the crash of falling slate, curses, and sudden terrified cries.

He was too young and inexperienced to think of rebelling against the fate which had plunged him into this horror. After a time he gave up trying to wash off the coal grime; he swallowed his food without tasting it. On Sundays, if the weather was good, he sat motionless in the little space behind the shack.

Only once did Ben Coleman manage to see him before the teacher left Malden. When the boy raised lackluster eyes rimmed about by coal dust, Coleman's voice nearly failed him. He laid his hand on the bowed shoulder and said earnestly, "Booker, you haven't come to the end of your schooling. This bad time will pass. Don't give up! When your father recovers, get out of that mine! Promise me, Booker!" the young man pleaded.

"What'll I do, sah?" Booker's voice was hoarse.

"Go to school! Some way, somehow, Booker, go to school!"

Booker looked down at his grimy hands, at the scars and cuts on his legs, and said nothing. But that night he tossed about on his cot. The next day a premature explosion of powder killed one miner and injured several others. Booker and John were thankful they escaped unhurt.

Tom was away from work six months. He returned with a slimp limp and was therefore considered of less value to the operators. He was given "lighter" work at reduced pay.

Coal mining was now the growing industry of West Virginia. Former salt makers turned their interest to the rapidly expanding mines. Men came to this section from other parts of the country seeking work. Mine owners brought in miners from Ireland. Fights were frequent and living conditions grew worse as another year went by.

Ben Coleman did not return to Malden. The old settlers deplored his absence. Once more the need of a school for Negroes was a topic of conversation, though nobody did anything about it until the Preacher started having evening classes at church.

One morning while riding out to the mine Booker could not help hearing an argument which almost flared into a fight between two Negro workers. The two were engaged in a low conversation when the boy climbed onto the truck. They moved over to make room for him and continued talking. Booker sank down in a corner as always, the driver cracked his whip, and the truck moved laboriously. Except for jolts and bumps of the cart the trip was usually made in heavy silence. It was still dark and some of the men dozed and nodded in their places. All conserved their energies for the long day ahead.

But this morning the two voices increased in volume until one of the Negroes exclaimed angrily, "What yo' talkin' 'bout? Plantin'! Who go tuh school to lea'n plantin'? Readin' an' writin's fo' mah chillin. Ah ain't hearin' nothin' 'bout no school what teaches 'em to plant co'n!"

"You's a fool!" retorted the other. "Dis hyeah school teach

readin' an writin' an' figgerin' long wid what else us needs tuh know. What yo' gonna eat while yo' readin' books? Eh? Yo' jus' tell me!"

"Aw, shut yo' big mouf! All yo' thinkin' 'bout is fillin' hit wid grub. Mah chillin's gonna get lea'nin' lak white folks. See?"

"Yeah? Dat's what yo' thinks! Well, mah boy at Hampton's lea'nin' how to build his own house, how to plant his own crops. An' he readin' all dis outta a book!"

The first man exploded into good-natured laughter. "Gowon, man! Yo' kills me! A book 'bout plantin' beans an' 'taters! What d' yo' all know 'bout dat?"

Snickers and derisive snorts acknowledged his inquiry. The second man relapsed into sullen silence.

Booker sat motionless, but what he had just heard was like a handful of peebles tossed into the deep well of his mind. Every pebble started a ripple of thought. By the time they reached the mine it was light enough for Booker to see the man who talked about the odd school. The boy managed to get near him as they walked to the mine entrance.

"Whar yo' from, mistah?" he asked.

"Ah'm from Hampton, sonny. Hampton Roads."

There was no time for anything more. A few minutes later Booker was going down, down, until darkness swallowed him up. But somehow the black depths did not seem so heavy. He could breathe.

It was several days, however, before Booker heard anything more about schools. Then he saw the newcomer waiting in line for his pay and managed to ride back to town in the same truck. The man answered questions readily enough.

"Sonny," he said as they separated on the corner, "Hampton's da school fo' our people! Boys lak yo' is comin' dar in droves an' da t'ings dey's lea'n'in' make yo' head swim. Yo' hyeah me, boy!"

His mother noticed that Booker's steps did not drag with fatigue that night. He flashed her a smile and ate his supper with apparent relish. Then, instead of flinging himself down on his cot, he pushed aside his bowl and asked, "Where's my books, Ma?"

She caught her breath in surprise but without a word reached up to a shelf and took down the Webster speller, the reader, and a folded newspaper with which Ben Coleman had supplemented his school's limited textbooks.

"Want yo' slate, honey?" she asked as she laid the neat pile on the table.

"No, ma'am, an' thanks." He moved the lighted tallow nearer and bent his head over the reader.

It had been many months since he had touched his schoolbooks. Now his forehead knotted in a frown and his lips moved as he struggled with the unfamiliar words.

Mandy watched him for a few minutes before asking, "Yo' goin' tuh school, Booker?"

"Yeah," he answered without looking up.

His mother's heart leaped. But as she opened her mouth to speak Tom stomped into the shack. She hastily set out her husband's supper. Mandy knew better than to ask further questions.

Several nights later Jane returned home after the other wage earners. She set a covered basket on the table and Mandy pounced upon it with cries of delight. It was filled with leftovers from a big dinner! Jane hung up her shawl and told them she had been called in to help the cook at "Mis' Ruffner's," adding triumphantly, "An' yo' all knows who *dat* is!"

They did, and could understand why Jane's face glowed with pride. General Lewis Ruffner was the owner of the coal mine. His house was by far the biggest and finest anywhere around. Booker listened attentively while his mother described the place.

"She got much help?" he asked.

Jane laughed. "Mostly ole folks—been wid 'em long time. Dat Mis' Ruffner so fussy can't nobody hardly please huh. Cook say dey needin' a handy man right now. Dat's why she had tuh get me for dis big party. Ain't got 'nuff help."

"She like yo', didn't she, Ma?" asked Booker.

His mother smiled. "Ah thinks she did, son. She seem mighty leased."

Booker grinned now. "Fine, Ma," he said eagerly, "yo' can

help me get the job. I wanna work fur Mis' Ruffner."

"What's dat?" Tom jerked his head.

"Yessah." Booker had to clear his throat. "I can't stay in the mines no longer, Pa. I gotta work outside—so I can go to school!"

It was out then and Booker waited for the explosion. Tom rubbed his hand along the upper part of the leg which always ached now. His broad, heavy face was filled with shadows as he sat a moment bent over in the chair. When he lifted his eyes they were somber.

"Ah reckon yo' right, boy." A deep sigh filled the pause. "Can't see hits much bettah dan slavery—diggin' in da ground all day—ain't much fur free man!" His head sank.

"Tom!" Jane moved swiftly to his side. She laid her broad hand on her husband's rounded shoulder; she spoke almost fiercely, "Don't say hit, Tom! We's free! Nothin' changes dat—an' we'll get ahead! Yo' see!"

The Ruffner cook heard Jane with sympathetic ears. She put in a good word for her to her lady, who agreed to take the boy on trial.

"You people are lazy and careless," the lady said sternly, "though your former masters are more to blame than you. If the boy is capable of learning I'll teach him. Yes, I'll give him a trial!"

"Thankee, ma'am," murmured Jane.

Mrs. Viola Ruffner was a native of Vermont who had married into a prominent Virginia family without shedding any of her austere Yankee attitudes. She considered all Southerners lazy and inefficient, the plantations miserably administered and utterly wasteful, and slavery the breeding ground for all the worst human tendencies. Her pity for the slaves was tinged with fear of them. She was certain now that only the most severe discipline would prevent the freed blacks from becoming criminals.

At her first sight of Booker, Mrs. Ruffner exclaimed in horror, "You're dirty! Go away and wash yourself thoroughly!"

Booker was much too big to cry, but tears stung his eyes as he stumbled back to the kitchen.

61

"I try so hard—coal dust won't come off," he told Lindy, the cook.

"Deed hit will," the stout woman declared cheerfully. "Yo' jus' come wid me to da wash shed. Ah'll show yo'!"

Pails of hot water in a big wooden tub—soft soap, dipped out of a pail—stiff brushes! Booker had never had such a bath before. He emerged from the suds with his body tingling and red, but every particle of the coal grime had disappeared.

"Now yo' can put on a pair of Jake's clean ovahalls," said Lindy, tossing him a coarse, faded garment. "Put yo' clothes in tub tuh soak!"

So Booker began his new job in borrowed clothes but with a clean, shining face. He applied himself most zealously. Mrs. Ruffner was a hard taskmaster and for a while Booker trembled whenever she called to him. But after a time he began to understand her demands. Everything must be kept clean; orders must be carried out promptly and systematically. He learned to answer her questions fully and frankly. He discovered that it was his job to keep every door, every fence and window in repair. He was expected to look around and *see what ought to do done*. In his *Up from Slavery*, Dr. Washington writes:

> The lessons I learned in the home of Mrs. Ruffner were as valuable to me as any education I have ever gotten anywhere since. Even to this day I never see bits of paper scattered around a house or in the street that I do not want to pick them up at once. I never see a filthy yard that I do not want to clean it, a paling off of a fence that I do not want to put it on, an unpainted or unwhitewashed house that I do not want to paint or whitewash it, or a button off one's clothes, or a grease-spot on them or on a floor, that I do not want to call attention to it.

Booker passed his trial period successfully. His pay was set at five dollars a month—half of this he gave to his mother; the other half was put away "to go to Hampton." When winter came and the weather turned unusually bad it was decided that

Booker should remain nights where he worked. Thus his induction into a new kind of life was complete. The boy had his own tiny room on the top floor of the Big House—a room which he must keep clean and neat. He took frequent hot baths in the shed, and the cook saw to it that he was well fed. There was more, much more. He heard speech such as he had never heard before, saw books and papers and journals lying on tables or standing in neat rows. He heard the word "library" for the first time and discovered that this was Mrs. Ruffner's favorite room. He invented reasons for going into this room: the fireplace needed logs—a window was rattling—the floor needed polishing.

The boy was awkward and he made many mistakes. But Mrs. Ruffner soon realized that he seldom made the same mistake twice and that he was honest. She tried him out on this last score, several times, by leaving small things lying about—even pieces of money. Booker never touched anything and after a while the lady relaxed her constant surveillance.

Booker had been with them several months when, one evening, Mrs. Ruffner said to her husband, "The mine boy is working out very well. He's really quite bright. I discovered today that he can read and write."

"That's fine, my dear," murmured her husband absently. Lewis Ruffner, who was still addressed as "General Ruffner," was a busy man. He was considering merging his coal mine with one farther west. The industry was growing almost too big for him to handle alone. He had not the vaguest idea what his wife had discovered. Whatever it was, she seemed satisfied and he was content.

"He says he wants to go to school, though schools for Negroes are surely still in the experimental stage. Somebody opened one here last year, but of course the Negroes didn't keep it up. They say the teacher didn't have enough pupils to keep open. This black boy says he wants to go to school. But will he stick to it? Of course he isn't really black, but he is—"

"Mrs. Ruffner," interrupted her husband irritably, "what in heavens name are you talking about?"

"I said that Booker, our hired boy, wants to go to school. He told me something about a school called Hampton. Have you ever heard of a school for Negroes at Hampton?"

General Ruffner's face flushed angrily. "That's where the Yankees set up a camp for runaway slaves! Their general called them 'contraband of war' and gave away free food, lodging, and protection to lure our slaves away. Now the section swarms with beggars, petty thieves, and lice!"

Mrs. Ruffner's face had flushed at the word Yankees. She spoke coldly, "Naturally I knew nothing of all this."

"Of course not, my dear," her husband said, his voice contrite. "But you must tell that boy not to be talking Hampton—or he'll be put off my place."

Mrs. Ruffner told Booker that Hampton had a "bad reputation" and let it go at that. By this time she was interested in the boy and didn't want him going off on a wild goose chase which might involve him in all kinds of trouble. Desiring, however, to encourage his obvious desire to improve himself, she made a generous offer.

"Booker," she said, "every morning when you've finished your chores you can spend an hour studying. I'll help you and allow you to take books from the shelves in the library."

As the months passed, Booker steadily improved. On his visits to the shack every member of the family regarded him with pride. One of their number was certainly getting ahead.

One evening about the middle of June an unexpected visitor arrived at the Ruffners' home. He was Dr. William H. Ruffner, Superintendent of Public Instruction in Virginia. Lindy was not yet ready to serve dinner, so Booker hastily put on a fresh coat and carried a tray of cool drinks out to the veranda.

"I *am* tired, Cousin Lewis," the visitor was saying as Booker stepped through the door. "I just came from the commencement at Hampton. I tell you that Hampton Normal and Agricultural Institute is something this old state can be proud of!" The visitor did not see Mrs. Ruffner's gesture of warning. His stentorious voice flowed over General Ruffner's snort. "What stronger evidence could be presented of the love of Virginia for learning than the fact that it cannot be quenched or suppressed by war or pinching poverty? Here we are, honestly and uncomplainingly shouldering the responsibility of educating our colored people!" The orator seized a glass from Booker's tray and held it high. "Here's to Virginia, sah—first, as always, in the right!"

After only a moment's hesitation the General reached for a glass. Mrs. Ruffner sat bolt upright in her chair. She did not drink spirituous liquors. Nobody noticed that Booker almost dropped the tray.

"That's all, boy!" said the General brusquely.

Booker hurried back to the kitchen. He was shaking with excitement.

"It's true!" he told startled Lindy. "True about Hampton! What the miner said—"

"Hush yo' mouf, boy, an' git dem dishes on the table!" the cook cut him off.

Booker knew they talked about Hampton throughout dinner. He heard the General's angry voice, and long speeches from his relative. But every time the boy came into the room with his tray they stopped talking. He felt their eyes on him as, with lowered eyes, he changed plates and brushed away crumbs. And when the door swung shut behind him argument was resumed.

With company in the house Booker did not presume to go near the library. After Dr. Ruffner drove away in the carriage the following afternoon, the boy went to the front of the house to put the rooms in order. As he was emptying the waste-paper basket in the library, something slipped to the floor. He stooped to pick it up and saw two lines of black letters staring up at him. He formed the words slowly: *Hamp-ton Nor-mal and Agri-cul-tural Institute.*

He held the sheet in his hand and gazed with wonder on a picture of a building finer than anything he had ever seen. There were rows of windows on top of each other, gables, and wide doors. From the top of a lofty steeple flew a flag far bigger than the one over Malden's post office. And along the walks in front of the building were men and women wearing hats and capes. They stood on the edge of shining water and looked up at the flag.

This was *Hampton*! Booker's hands trembled as he turned

65

the folder. It was an announcement about the school, setting forth its purpose; naming its teachers and inviting students for the next session, which began "Sept. 15th, 1872."

Booker could not read all the finely printed lines, but he had seen enough. With a guilty look over his shoulder he stuffed the folder inside his shirt and gathered up the trash.

Mrs. Ruffner's stern conscience told her she ought to talk to the boy, ought to tell him about the school their kinsman recommended so highly. But she saw no possibility of the boy's going to it. Such an undertaking took money. Where could this boy get money? She had no money of her own and dared not mention the subject to her husband. The idea of *giving* money to the boy would probably undermine his character. He was really doing very well, she told herself. No doubt he had forgotten all about that business of going away to school. Even if he had overheard some of Dr. Ruffner's talk he would hardly grasp its significance. She resolved to have him read for her again some morning.

Booker was making his plans. At his first opportunity he went to his mother. The whole family gathered round and examined the Hampton folder. John had just had a slight raise at the mine.

"Ah give yo' da raise, Booker boy," he said. "Dat'll help."

Jane said she would speak to the Preacher. "Brothah Johnson know whar da school an' how yo' gits dar."

Tom patted his leg and growled, "Ole leg's holdin' out fine, son. Ah thought Ah finished while back. Ah'm goin' strong now."

And Mandy informed all, "Ah goin' tuh school lak Booker."

Soon the word circulated through Shantytown and among the old settlers. Negroes were pleased and proud. Old folks who had spent the best days of their lives in slavery hardly expected to live to see the time when a member of their race would leave home to attend a boarding school. They called to Booker when he passed by and gave him a nickel, a quarter, a handkerchief—something "tuh help, sonny."

Booker's savings had been reduced by the purchase of shoes and a few other things which his mother had not been able to acquire from castoffs. He had exactly twenty-two dollars and fifty cents. But he still had two months to work before September. He began wondering if there was any way he might increase his five-dollar wage. He hesitatingly approached Mrs. Ruffner on this problem.

That lady listened with tight lips. She asked, "Why do you need more money, Booker?"

The long, level look told her. "I'm goin' to school, ma'am. An' I—"

"Very well," she cut him off. "You may paint the fences. For that I'll pay you a dollar extry."

The summer passed too quickly. In spite of the help from Reverend Johnson's flock and from neighbors, Booker's meager funds did not keep pace with the calendar. Yet the boy's determination did not flag. When told that Hampton was five hundred miles from Malden, on the eastern shore of Virginia, he merely asked how often the stagecoaches went in that direction. He was certain he could find work when he reached the vicinity of Norfolk. He had learned that there were shipyards there. And Norfolk was very close to Hampton.

But in the midst of final preparations his mother fell ill. This was a blow which threatened everything.

"No, son, no," gasped Jane painfully. "Yo' goin'! Yo' Ma wantta see yo' go!"

He knelt beside her cot, holding her feverish hand. Doubts and fears tore at his heart. What if he should never see her again? For the first time he realized that he had planned to go far away and leave them all!

The next morning she was undoubtedly better. She smoothed and patted the little pile of his clothing all clean and pressed for him. Neighbors ran in and out of the shack all that summer evening. A festive air hung over everything. There was the smell of good food in the air as they shared what they had in a going-away "pahty fur Booker."

That night after everybody had gone Booker heard his mother calling him. Tom had gone out to the pump in the yard. Mother and son were alone.

"Booker," she said softly, "Ah wanna tell yo' somethin'

67

'portant. We all got a name now—lak yo' say—Washington; but Ah gotta tell yo' dat—yo' name—yo' real Pa's name is Taliaferro. Say hit, son!"

"Taliaferro," he repeated after her.

"Thankee, son," she murmured. "Now go sleep!"

The great day dawned bright and clear. Tom and John went off to the mine after telling him good-bye. His mother was too weak to accompany him to the stage depot, but Reverend Johnson and several of the neighbors went along and Mandy clasped his hand tightly while she skipped by his side. His other hand carried a small, cheap satchel.

Other passengers for the stagecoach regarded the oddly assorted group with some amusement. "Those people are so demonstrative," they thought as Booker's friends waved and shrilly called out, "Gawd bless yo', boy!". . ."Us pray fur yo'!" . . ."Bye-bye!"

The stagecoach turned the corner and Booker settled back in his seat. The world outside the window blurred before his eyes as for one moment loneliness engulfed him. Then he took a grip on himself, set his teeth, and whispered, "I'm going to Hampton Institute, and my name is Booker Taliaferro Washington."

Part II

GO DOWN, MOSES

<hr />

Is true Freedom but to break
Fetters for our own dear sake,
And with leathern hearts forget
That we owe mankind a debt?
No! true Freedom is to share
All the chains our brothers wear,
And with heart and hands to be
Earnest to make others free!

—James Russell Lowell

6

Hampton Institute

The story of Hampton Institute goes back to the year 1861, when the creek upon which Hampton stands was for a while the boundary line between two armies: the Union lines remained intrenched upon its eastern shore during the early part of the war, while the combating forces swayed back and forth as fortune favored one or the other. The town and the bridge across the creek were burned, and the few houses of richer residents which escaped the general destruction were made the headquarters of Union or Confederate officers, as might be. Beginning early in the summer of 1861, bands of Negroes came pouring in from the interior of the state and from the northern counties of North Carolina. They fled as the Israelites of old in little squads; by families, singly, or by whole plantations they flocked within the lines protected by Fortress Monroe. They put up hastily built cabins of split logs and squatted there on the land close beside the big guns. In August the American Missionary Association sent the Reverend C. L. Lockwood as a missionary to these black people who had chosen freedom. There, already working among them, he discovered Mrs. Mary S. Peake.

She was a wiry little brown woman with keen black eyes and tireless energy. She had already organized "reading classes" which were always overcrowded. Reverend Lockwood established Sunday schools and then appealed to his Association for primers and teachers that they might open weekday schools. In the fall a day school was opened in the deserted mansion of ex-President Tyler, in Hampton, with Mrs. Peake as the sole teacher. The Missionary Association soon sent help. Reports of the Negroes' eagerness for knowledge brought more teachers, but in April, 1862, Mrs. Peake died. Reverend Lockwood reported that this woman had literally laid down her life for her people, for "whom she labored beyond her strength until death lifted her self-imposed burden."

Miss Mary F. Mackie, teacher of mathematics and Enrollment Secretary of Hampton Normal and Agricultural Institute, know this story well. She knew that teachers at Hampton were still laboring far beyond their strength, but she, like Mary Peake, was quite willing to give her life that a people might live.

This morning she was preparing a report to the American Missionary Association and she was torn between justifiable pride in the Institute's good works and the sore necessity for stressing its needs. More new students had enrolled for this fall session than at the beginning of any other year. Nearly all of last year's students had come back. Despairingly she knew that this was only the beginning. How many they had been forced to turn away last year because the buildings were full! All through the chill of the Virginia winter, boys in squads of twenty-four to thirty at a time had lodged in tents whose canvas walls were frail protection against the stormy winds which visited their open seacoast. Behind her, on the office wall, hung an architect's picture of big, new Virginia Hall. But outside on the green slope overlooking the water were only the foundations. The building had been started last year. There was no money to finish it this year! Harvest from the farm had been good, very good; but the market—

A light tap on the door interrupted her thoughts. "Come in," called Miss Mackie. She lifted her nearsighted blue eyes as a neatly dressed student attendant entered and said, "Miss Mackie, a boy to see you."

"What does he want, Sarah?"

"He wants to enroll, ma'am. But, Miss Mackie, he ain't got—" She corrected herself hastily, "Ma'am, *he's got fifty cents!*"

"Tell him to wait, Sarah. I'll see him as soon as I finish this report."

She sighed as the girl closed the door. Always the same thing —no money. She would have to find a way, as that other Mary had done more than a decade ago—dark-skinned Mary S. Peake. With a quick glance at the clock Miss Mackie finished the report, laid the sheets together, and pushed back her chair. It was almost time for chapel services. She hurried into the adjoining room.

The big boy slouched on the bench was not a pretty sight. He was dirty and disheveled; his clothes were streaked and spotted. The fact that his shoes were old and broken did not count against him, but the mud on them might have been removed!

Miss Mackie's tone was sharp. "Well, young man!"

The boy gave a start, almost fell off the bench, and lifted red, bleary eyes. Then he stumbled to his feet. Miss Mackie's nose wrinkled in disgust.

Booker heard the Yankee twang in the white lady's voice and his heart sank. She would send him away because he was dirty! His last bed had been under the sidewalks in Richmond. For the past two days and nights he had been on the final lap of his journey to Hampton—coming part of the way down the James River in a fishing boat, the rest of the way on foot. It was the fish Miss Mackie smelled. He knew he looked like a tramp!

"What do you want here?" she asked.

"Ma'am—I come—to school." His voice was hoarse, but Miss Mackie caught the better diction.

"Where are you from?"

"I come from Malden, ma'am."

"Malden?"

"Yessum, Malden, West Virginnie—awful long ways, ma'am—five hundred miles—I come." There was a desperate pounding in his throat. *Please, lady, understand how far I come—understand how my money ran out—understand how many places I had to work to get here!* He wanted to shout all this, but the words caught in his throat. He could only plead with his eyes.

Miss Mackie had traveled five hundred miles south from

73

Massachusetts. Her well-bred, restricted imagination could not possibly picture this boy's odyssey, but she was impressed. He *had* come a long way.

Through the open window came the sound of a bell ringing. Time for chapel! Miss Mackie spoke quickly, "Come with me!"

He seized his satchel and followed her out of the office, down the hall a few doors, and into a big room with desks, benches, and *writing on the walls.* Booker's delighted gaze jerked away from this writing when the lady opened a narrow door and said crisply, "This recitation room needs cleaning. You'll find broom and dustcloths in this closet. Take the broom and sweep." Then she went out, leaving him alone.

Booker took a long, deep breath. The load was gone. She was giving him a trial! His face broke into a broad grin. *This was something he could do.* He put down his bag and went to work.

He swept the recitation room three times. This done, he took the dustcloth and went over every bit of woodwork around the walls; every bench, table, and desk. He moved every piece of furniture; cleaned every closet, every corner. He looked for and found a trash bin at the end of the hall. He carried out his sweepings and once more dusted everything with his cloth. He wiped long and hard.

When Miss Mackie returned after chapel service she found the boy standing in the middle of the room slowly turning about. He stood motionless while she inspected what he had done. She looked at the floor; she opened the closets; she walked about the room. Finally she paused beside the big desk up front, reached into her pocket and drew out a white cambric handkerchief. He watched, trembling, while the lady rubbed this clean handkerchief over the desk, along a bench, and across the back of a chair. She looked down at the handkerchief, shook it out, and examined it. Only then did she look at the applicant. There was no smile on her face, and her voice was as crisp as before.

"You'll do, young man," Miss Mackie said, and he heard the Yankee twang sing in her voice.

So, in the fall of 1872, Booker enrolled at Hampton and was given a job as janitor. His age was put down as fifteen. He was assigned to courses in reading, spelling, arithmetic, natural philosophy, geography, and history of the United States. He was to do supervised work on the farm and learn something of soil formation, drainage, and rotation of crops.

The rising bell rang at five-thirty. Every hour of the day thereafter was strictly scheduled until the retiring bell at nine-thirty. He was among the youngest of the students. Most of them were men and women—earnest men and women bent on making the most of every hour at Hampton. Some were too old and worn to master the textbooks, but there was much else for them to learn. They bent every effort to learn new and better ways—of cleanliness, of caring for children, of raising and cooking food. All burned with the desire to pass on their knowledge; all were preparing themselves to teach and lift up their people at home. Teachers and students alike joined in this effort. And, drawing them together in this noble purpose, supervising, guiding, directing, and inspiring was the genius of Hampton Institute, General Samuel Chapman Armstrong.

Booker did not see the principal that first day. It was a day filled with gratifying discoveries. When he lay down on his clean, narrow cot he was convinced that Hampton was well worth any sacrifice. The next morning when he was directed to his place for six-thirty "Family Prayer" he knew that the tall, distinguished figure on the platform could be none other than the head of the school. The man was every inch a soldier, commanding in aspect and bearing, with flashing black eyes under heavy brows, a sweeping forehead, and thick steel-gray hair. When the hall was absolutely still, this noble personage sank to his knees like the humblest of suppliants.

"Heavenly Father"—he spoke as to a loving friend and his voice became a melody that filled the room—"we thank Thee for Thy manifold goodness. Thou hast brought us safely through the night to this day filled with opportunity for service. Thou hast guided us this far on our way, hast blessed our efforts. We, Thy little children, praise Thee—praise Thee in spirit and in truth." . . .

All over the hall low, rich voices joined in forming an accompaniment to the prayer: "Hear us, Jesus!" . . . "Thank ye, Lawd.". . ."Aye, Lawd, yo' so good!"

Booker had never heard a white man pray with so much fervor. He had never before seen whites and blacks kneeling together. He looked out over the bowed heads, saw tears on the sunken cheeks of an old woman; and out of half-forgotten memories came the sound of singing on another morning at dawn, his mother's face streaming with tears and her voice shouting, *We free! Thank God, we free!*

The prayer this morning was followed by a song. Booker had never heard it before. As the simple lines were repeated in the changing cadence, he soon picked up the words. Many of the Negroes in the hall had been "contrabands" of war; they had fled before pursuing armies; they had huddled within the sound and smell of the big guns. So now they sang with passionate ardor:

> "Gwine tuh lay down mah sword an' shield
> Down by da ribber side,
> Down by da ribber side.
> Ain't gwine tuh study war no mo',
> Ah ain't gwine tuh study war no mo'—
> No mo'— No mo'— No mo'!
> Down by da ribber side,
> Down by da ribber side,
> Gwine tuh lay down mah sword an' shield
> An' study war no mo'!"

A people who can sing like this will surely rise! thought the principal. He looked down at the shining faces and his mind flashed back to the missionary father in the far-off Hawaiian Islands who had so richly endowed his son for the task before him. Samuel C. Armstrong had inherited the fearless evangelistic spirit of his parents. He had brought to Hampton from Hawaii the system of education based on manual labor which had been introduced by his father, and with remarkable success, into the public instruction of the Hawaiians.

The son's education had been entirely in his father's hands

76

until, at the age of twenty-one, Samuel Armstrong was sent to a New England college at Williamstown, Massachusetts. He was graduated from Williams College in the summer of 1862 and went immediately into the army. A year later he was Colonel of the Eighth Regiment of U. S. Colored Troops. When the Freedmen's Bureau was set up for the benefit of destitute ex-slaves, the then Brigadier-General Armstrong became one of its chief officials. At Hampton, where he was stationed, efforts were being made to bring schooling to the hundreds of Negroes gathered there, and General Armstrong gave what assistance he could to the men and women working under the direction of the American Missionary Association. In 1867 he published an article in the *American Missionary Magazine* in which he pleaded with the entire country to aid by every means possible. In clear, eloquent language he stated the needs of the recently freed black people.

The country as a whole would benefit, said General Armstrong, if the freedmen were trained as swiftly as possible to fit themselves for the demands and responsibilities of free men. Not only was "book learning" necessary, but the far broader teaching of a free, yet disciplined life: self-respect, industry, punctuality and, above all, the *dignity of labor*. Teachers of their own race must be prepared—young men and women who could go out among them and, as heads of primary schools, could control and lead the children, while, by the influence of their orderly, intelligent lives, they could at the same time influence the moral and physical condition of the parents.

As the result of this article, philanthropists and public-spirited citizens throughout the land joined with the American Missionary Association in urging General Armstrong to head such a school at Hampton. Events moved rapidly and, in the fall of 1868, Hampton Normal and Agricultural Institute was founded. Four years had passed and now, as the song died away, the principal thought, *We've a long ways to go but, thank God, we're on our way!*

A loud chord on the small organ. The students turned about sharply. Then, as a stirring strain sounded valiantly, they began to march.

These were his soldiers now! General Armstrong snapped to

attention. "Heads up! Eyes front!" he commanded. Booker threw back his shoulders. His pulse leaped and his blood tingled as his feet picked up the rhythm. He swung round a corner and his eyes met those of the tall man on the platform. In spite of himself a broad grin flashed across the boy's face. It was gone in an instant, but the principal had seen it.

Though he was not sure of every name in the new class, General Armstrong prided himself on knowing his students. Yet surely here was a face he had not seen before.

"Who is that boy?" he asked the teacher standing behind him. "The one crossing the side aisle?"

Mr. Howe, teacher of agriculture, took a step forward the better to see.

"Oh, sir," he said immediately, "he just came. I believe his name is Franklin—no," he corrected himself, "it's Washington."

Samuel C. Armstrong looked after the boy stumbling through the door. He stared after the new arrival who would someday make his method of education famous. He looked after the student whose application of his manual-training methods would influence the entire course of education, not only in the United States, but throughout the world, and he said, "That boy's got a good head. We must keep our eye on him!"

◇◇◇◇◇◇◇◇◇◇◇◇◇◇◇◇◇◇ 7 ◇◇◇◇◇◇◇◇◇◇◇◇◇◇◇◇◇◇

The Student Teacher

Springtime is lovely on the eastern shores of Virginia. After soft April showers the lowlands between the York and James rivers had burst into trailing flowers. Salt air blowing in from Hampton Roads picked up the fragrance, and the one hundred and ninety acres called Hampton Institute quivered with new life.

Because of his janitor duties Booker arose an hour before the five-thirty rising bell. As Miss Mackie had anticipated, the steady arrival of new students had crowded out the sleeping quarters. Booker with other volunteers had moved into tents which stood in neat rows along the slope. This morning Booker pushed back the flap of the old army tent and, standing erect, looked across sparkling waters to where the sun blazed on the horizon. Several fishing boats bobbed among the golden waves, their white sails flapping in the morning breeze as they made their way homeward with the night's catch. Farther out, a large vessel slowly moved through the straits. Booker drew in a deep breath of the exhilarating air. His eyes glowed as he looked after the ship.

"Someday," he whispered, "I'm going out to sea on a big ship!" He shook himself and laughed silently, then set off across the dewy ground to the main building.

Hampton had filled the boy's head with dreams. Life was good and anything was possible! Yet nobody at Hampton Institute pampered him. Tight-lipped Yankee teachers made stern demands. They spared neither themselves nor those who came to them. Having themselves been trained in the best colleges of the land and some being from old families of wealth and culture, Hampton's teachers maintained very high standards. They were quite willing to adapt their teaching to the needs of a people so recently in slavery, but these eighteen devoted, consecrated men and women were determined that freedmen must shoulder responsibilities and must enter the arena of free men prepared to compete and achieve without apologies or special concessions.

Booker could not go home at the end of his first year. He had no money for the long trip and he owed the institution sixteen dollars that he had not been able to work out. His usual soaring spirits flagged as other students and teachers left for home. He tried to conceal his feelings in the midst of their excitement and happy anticipation, but his heart was heavy as he cleaned the empty classrooms. He had to go somewhere, since only a small crew of skilled farmers remained at Hampton Institute during the summer. He nevertheless wrote a cheerful letter to his mother, with messages for all, and sent it, as always, to Reverend Johnson.

After trying for several days to find a job in the town of Hampton, Booker secured work in a restaurant at Fortress Monroe. His wages were little more than his board, but at night and between meals he found considerable time for study and reading. He also took advantage of the summer to see some of the surrounding country, which he read about in his history book.

He climbed up into the fortress and from its turrets looked out over Chesapeake Bay. A soldier pointed across the mouth of the James River to the ruins of Jamestown, where the first shipload of slaves was landed in 1619. In the town of Hampton, Booker stood before the quaint little church of St. John, built between 1660 and 1667; he visited the suburb called Slabtown, where a remnant of the great host of runaway slaves still inhabited ramshackle cabins and existed in poverty and filth; he walked around great houses of former rich slaveholders—houses now deserted and falling into decay. Then he returned to Hampton Institute, sincere testimonial of heroic effort on the part of white and black people, where old things had passed away and new hopes blossomed for the future.

Booker progressed rapidly during his second year at Hampton. Teachers gave scant praise, but they were quick to recognize capabilities. Miss Nathalie Lord, teacher of reading, heard how well this student handled words and gave him private lessons in breathing, articulation, and emphasis. She opened her Bible and had him read aloud certain of the Psalms and Songs of Solomon; she suggested his admittance to the Debating Society, which was made up of men much older. John Larry, whose home was in Rochester, New York, called Booker to assist in the printing room.

One day Mr. Larry said, "Booker, I want to show you something valuable."

He opened a drawer and took out a folded newspaper, opened it up, and spread it on the table. "See here!"

Booker read the title aloud: *The North Star.* He looked up. "That's a strange name for a newspaper, sir," he said.

"It is, isn't it?" agreed Mr. Larry. "Well, this newspaper was one of the most powerful organs in the country for freeing the slaves. Its publisher and printer was a man of your own race, a Negro named Frederick Douglass."

The boy leaned over the newspaper and eagerly scanned the sheet. The date was June 13, 1850. A faint pencil line drew his eyes to one column.

"Let's hear how well you can read that aloud, Booker," suggested the teacher.

Booker read easily:

"Wherein does the white man differ from the black? Why, one is white and the other is black. What of that? Does the sun shine more brilliantly upon the one than it does upon the other? Do earth, sea and air yield their united treasures to the one more readily than to the other? In a word, have we not all one Father? The Negro stands erect. Upon his brow he bears the seal of manhood from the hand of the living God. Adopt any mode of reasoning you please, he is a man, possessing an immortal soul, illuminated by intellect, capable of heavenly aspirations, and in all things pertaining to manhood, he is at once self-evidently a man, and therefore entitled to all the rights and privileges which belong to human nature. . . ."

Booker looked up and his eyes wavered. "That's—that's—" he stammered, and stopped. He had no words to express his whirling thoughts. Indeed he was afraid to try. He suddenly distrusted the white man.

Perhaps the teacher sensed something of the conflict in the boy's mind. He folded the paper carefully and said, "You might be interested in some of this material for your debates. Frederick Douglass is famous now and lives in Washington, D. C.; but for many years he lived in Rochester, just a few blocks from my home. I've often seen him. Indeed I attended the same school as his boys."

"The *same* school?" Booker could not believe his own ears.

"Yes, Booker, the same school." He replaced the paper in

the drawer. "Now then," he said briskly, "set up the type for those concert programs, and be sure you spell Mr. Fenner's name with two *n*'s."

For the next hour Booker painstakingly chose letters from the inky type box and arranged them within printing blocks. And all the time he was thinking of another member of his race who published a *newspaper! A famous Negro!*

Booker's farm work that year was with livestock. He learned that fine stock was the result of breeding and correct care. He applied the theories so well that one of his pigs took a prize at the spring showing—a prize which carried with it ten dollars. The young breeder's cup of joy was brimful. He wrote home that this summer he would see them.

Reverend Johnson had written urging him to come home for the summer. His mother was not well and was longing for him. John promised to send extra money toward his expense. His brother had been sending all he could spare at regular intervals. Booker knew what any extra effort would mean. His prize money would carry him a long way toward Malden.

All work increased as commencement approached. This was the time when scores of visitors came to the school: trustees, educators, capitalists who might make much-needed gifts, philanthropists, anxious friends, and critics. Everything had to be spick-and-span. Teachers and students toiled far into the night.

At midnight on the last Saturday before the commencement programs were laid out to dry, John Larry wiped his hands on the blackened towel hanging behind the door. He had sent all his helpers except Booker to bed two hours ago.

He looked over at the boy, who was picking up trash from the floor, and said, "We'll lock the door against inspection, Booker. I'll clean that up tomorrow. Let's go to bed!"

Booker threw him a quick smile. "It won't take me long to sweep it up, Mr. Larry."

"No, I want to lock up." He took his coat off the hook and put it on. "Well, this was our last job. We'll soon be going home!" He blew out the oil lamp on the table. Moonlight pouring in through the window showed them the way out.

The long hallway was dark, but soon they were out in the

sweet June night. As they parted near a clump of trees the teacher handed the boy an envelope, saying, "Things get so hectic the last couple of days, Booker, I might not see you again. Here's something for your faithful services to the printing department. I hope you have a good summer. Good night!" He turned off down the path.

"Good night, and thank you kindly, sir." In the envelope were five one-dollar bills.

Six days later Booker, accompanied by two other students, boarded the westbound train in Richmond. They made a quiet, orderly trio—young men already thinking of themselves as "leaders" of their race, endowed with a deep sense of responsibility, and anxious to make a good impression on all the world. They parted at Lynchburg, where Booker took a stagecoach going northwest and the other two went on to Kentucky.

In due time the lumbering stagecoach reached Malden, and Booker hurried home through the dusk as fast as the heavy suitcase at his side would allow. His mother cried for joy when she saw him in the doorway. He leaped across the room and held her in his arms. Tom watched with a broad smile, while outside at the pump Mandy heard his voice and came running. Then, suddenly, the shack was full!

"Lookee he fine clothes!" somebody exclaimed with awesome admiration.

The clothes had come from missionary barrels sent to Hampton, but women students had mended and refitted each garment so that every seam was in place and not a button missing. They pointed at his polished shoes and whistled.

Booker's light laugh was calculated to hide his dismay at sight of the bent, shrunken form of his mother. Her hair had receded from her face until there remained only sparse patches of gray; her face was gaunt. Only her eyes were the same. And Tom, too, whom he remembered as big and sturdy, seemed small and wavering.

Mandy, however, was a big girl with long, skinny legs, and when John walked into the shack the two brothers exclaimed almost simultaneously, "Fellow! Yo' big ox!" Never before had they laughed so heartily.

Out of the suitcase came something for each one: things made by the students at Hampton and sold for a few pennies, but each gift was received with shouts of delight. Booker had not, however, prepared for a new member of the family.

In the midst of the babble of talk, his mother suddenly exclaimed, "Jimmy boy, come on in! Lan's sakes, Ah clean forgot!"

A thin barefoot boy, who had been peeping around the side of the door, now shyly entered. He was seven or eight years old. He sidled up to Jane, his eyes lifted trustingly to her worn face.

"Booker," she said, laying her hand on the boy's head, "this hyear's yo' lil brothah." When Booker blinked his eyes in amazement, the neighbors joined in her laughter. "We 'dopted him," she explained. "Now we all his family. Tell Booker yo' name, honey!"

The boy looked up and declared firmly, "James B. Washin'ton—dat's mah full name."

"His folks all dead," whispered John in Booker's ear.

"Well, Jimmy, how do you do!" Booker gravely shook hands. "Do you know my name?"

"Sho' do—yo's Booker Washin'ton."

"Booker *Taliaferro* Washington," corrected Booker, lifting his eyes to his mother, whose lips quivered with a smile.

"Dat's too much!" said the boy, grinning broadly.

Booker soon learned why Tom and John were at home— why so many men were walking or standing about in Shantytown. Not a salt furnace in the county was operating and, just three days before, the miners had gone out on strike.

This was something new to Negro workers. The mines had given most of them their first wages. No matter how small that wage was or what the conditions under which they worked, they wanted to keep on working and drawing pay. Tom railed bitterly at "lousy furriners" with their "crazy talk." Neighbors joined him by loudly denouncing "agitators."

Booker's heart sank. He managed to get John outside, and said, "Ma looks bad. Was she down sick?"

John shook his head. "Ma won' stay down. She jus' ailin' all

84

da time. She worryin' 'bout da strike. Ah'm awful sorry 'bout dis—fur yo', Booker."

Booker took his brother's arm; his voice trembled. "You're the best brother in the world, John. I feel terrible at how you all been working for me." He tried to clear his throat but could not. "I'll make—it up—to you, boy. I'm pitching in this summer with—all I got."

Early the next morning he set out to find a job. Confidence in himself was high. He had "learnin'." He went straight to the town square. Most of the tradesmen, shopkeepers, and managers regarded the rather "impudent boy" with some curiosity. They had no work for him. The Negro barber greeted him cordially.

"Sho', I heard tell 'bout you. Went off to school! Well, well!" He cocked his head admiringly. Then he pursed his mouth. "Can you barber?"

"I can learn, Mr. Wells," Booker declared. "At Hampton we—"

The barber waved him to silence. "Can' take no 'prentice in here, son. I has the most 'portant people in this county." He paused impressively. "My customers mighty particular, I can tell you." He tapped his head thoughtfully. "Now, maybe George Peters could take you on. He's a carpenter—right around the corner. You'll see his sign. Come see us sometime, young man. Me an' my wife would love to hear 'bout that school. Come have dinner with us!"

George Peters declared that he would gladly hire such a promising student if he had anything for him to do.

"Nobody's buildin' nothin' in dis town no more." He shook his bald head sadly. "Malden ain't lak hit use to be. Tell me 'bout dat school, young man! Ah got two boys myself."

Nat Calvert, who ran a livery stable on the next corner, regarded Booker with some suspicion until he told who he was. The black man's white teeth showed in a wide grin.

"Hit's nice of yo' to come an' see me." He looked around at his big, crowded stable. "Reverend Johnson tell us 'bout yo' at church. Now—no fine young man lak yo' wan's to work in dis hyear dirty place."

"That's where you're wrong, Mr. Calvert. Work is honorable. You own this place. I'd be glad to work for you."

"Yo' would, boy?" The broad face beamed. "Well, business mighty bad jus' now; but Ah'll be proud tuh take yo' on soon as things pick up. Yessah, Ah'd be mighty proud!"

Malden was in a slump. Nobody was hiring. Before returning home Booker stopped at Reverend Johnson's house. He was not at home, this being a day he spent in Parkersville. His wife invited Booker in, pressed a piece of pie on him, and plied him with questions about Hampton.

"Reverend'll be so glad to see you, Booker," she told him. "We all proud of you!"

Within the next few days Booker presented himself, respectfully but insistently, at the back door of every Big House in the area. He began by going to see Mrs. Ruffner.

Lindy, the cook, did not recognize the stranger tapping on her kitchen door. When he took off his cap she gave a whoop of pleasure and pulled him inside. Mrs. Ruffner, too, was pleasantly surprised to see her former house boy and to learn that he had been at school for the past two years.

"How ever did you manage it?" she asked.

"I, and my family, worked very hard," answered Booker.

"Well, evidently the school has done you good," conceded Mrs. Ruffner. "And now what?"

Her face clouded when Booker told her he was looking for work.

"I'm afraid I couldn't—Mr. Ruffner's very upset about the strike, you know. He doesn't blame your people," she added hastily. "They only suffer from the agitation stirred up by outsiders. But this situation makes it difficult for all of us."

Reverend Johnson told him things were not so critical in Parkersville.

"They don't depend so much on coal mines and saltworks. I'm sure we could find a job for you in Parkersville."

Booker was reluctant to go fifty miles away from home, but after further futile attempts this seemed the only course open. Reverend Johnson drove his own two-wheeled gig there and back every week. Booker told him he would like to go to Parkersville on his next trip.

The Preacher agreed willingly. Then he said, "I wonder, Booker, if you would come to church before you go and tell us something about Hampton Institute."

Booker blinked his eyes. "You mean"—he gulped—"talk in church?"

Reverend Johnson smiled. "You've been talking plenty at school. What about your Debating Society?" His eyes grew serious. "Such a talk would mean a great deal to our people. It's pretty hard going right now. I fear some of them are doubting God's goodness. You've been someplace—you've seen something. Let me circulate the word around that Booker Washington will speak Sunday. Young and old will come. They all know about you and they're proud of you." He leaned forward. "You owe it to them, Booker. From what you've told me of Hampton, I think that's what those back there would want you to do."

Booker swallowed. The Preacher was right. "Duty" was the watchword at Hampton. The boy now recognized this call to duty.

"All right," he said huskily. "All right, sir, I'll speak."

Jane was up early the following Sunday morning. All the family was going to church. Booker heard his mother humming as she worked. Jimmy ran out to the pump a dozen times and Mandy brushed her hair with relentless vigor. All around them neighbors were stirring with equal determination—for on that day most of Shantytown trooped across the town to the African Methodist Episcopal Church.

Old settlers from neat cottages and transit workers from Shantytown, some in "plantation jeans," smiled at one another as they pushed into the rough benches. They were all Negroes. They were all proud of "Mis' Washin'ton's boy." So they blended their voices in lusty song, meekly bowed their heads while Preacher Johnson laid their cause before the Great White Throne, then folded their hands complacently and sat back to listen.

Facing them on the platform, Booker heard himself being introduced in words he scarcely recognized. He shifted his feet nervously; his throat was dry, his tongue stiff. The Preacher's voice stopped. Booker saw him turn and make a gesture toward him. Now was the time for him to get up. But he could not move.

"We're waiting for you, Booker." Reverend Johnson's low, encouraging voice pulled him to his feet. He staggered toward the pulpit clutching in his right hand the sheets upon which he had conscientiously written his "speech." For a moment the faces swam before his eyes. He could distinguish nothing.

Clearing his throat, he blurted desperately, "Brothers and Sisters—" This was the proper beginning for a church speech. This was what he had written down. But now he could not see the lines on the sheet. With both hands he clung to the pulpit and shut his eyes.

Those watching thought he prayed. And perhaps the effort Booker made was a prayer. For, in that moment, past, present, and future seemed to meet. The full mantle of responsibility enveloped him—never to be thrown off. In that moment he told himself, *My people are waiting. They are waiting for me— for me!*

He opened his eyes and saw them—saw each dark, lifted face; saw the shadows and lines, saw the patient mouths, saw the eager light in their eyes.

He leaned toward them and said, "People of my race—I have been given the opportunity to go to a school which prepares me for service. Many of you helped me. I thank you from the bottom of my heart." All the faces swayed toward him, giving him confidence. He talked now to a group of warm friends. "Hampton Institute is a wonderful school. It would take me a long time to tell you all they've taught me at Hampton. But I know now that you, my own people, have given me more than any school can give."

He saw his mother's eyes fill with tears, saw the splotches of coal on his brother's face twitch, saw his stepfather shift his bad leg.

"And this is something I pray God I'll never forget. You have taught me that freedom is worth any price we are called upon to pay. You have taught me how to endure and suffer without complaint—how to work for little reward—how to have great faith. What I learned at Hampton I can now add to what you already know. We don't go to Hampton to get away from work but to learn how to work better. They teach that hard work is good. That means that my people who do the hardest work are the best. They teach that God intended for man to work with his hands. Therefore our rough, scarred hands are beautiful to Him."

He paused and wet his lips. For ten or fifteen minutes more he told them about Hampton—told of his work, of his classes, of how the white teachers worked with their students, of how his pig won a prize. They listened, with only an occasional murmur of approbation or a low-voiced "Bless 'im, Jesus!"

Remembering General Armstrong's fervent exhortations, Booker concluded with these words: "God has brought us out of slavery. I know He will carry us on our way if we put our trust in Him and in ourselves."

The little church was filled with a rustling sigh as he took his seat. Booker T. Washington had made his first speech. It was the only speech his mother was to hear. But perhaps he never made a better one.

Jane was a queen that day. For it was her hand they wrung. "A fine boy, Sistah Washin'ton!". . ."Ain't yo' proud, Sistah Washin'ton!" . . . "Gawd bless dat boy, Sistah Washin'ton!" It was the happiest day of her life.

They were almost shy with him. The tall, gray-eyed young man was a miracle. For the most part they gaped at him in wonder.

But Reverend Johnson said solemnly, "My boy, God has surely laid His hand on you."

Early the next morning Booker set off with Reverend Johnson for Parkersville. It was afternoon when they arrived and Booker's first efforts were fruitless. They spent the night at the home of a parishioner. The next day Booker was hired as janitor for a new building which would be ready for occupancy the following Monday. He could, therefore, return with the Preacher for a few more days at home.

"I don't like traveling the roads alone after dark," said Reverend Johnson, but this evening the time passed rapidly. Neither noticed clouds gathering behind them in the hills. The storm broke suddenly. They took refuge in an abandoned house on the side of the road. As the winds howled and the rain came down in torrents Reverend Johnson told him, "We're only a few miles from home, but I fear the bridge will be washed away. Best stay here until daylight."

The dawn gave every promise of a perfect June day. The freshly cleansed countryside was beautiful, but the gig wheels sank in the mud and they made slow progress. The bridge was washed away. They had to travel several miles downstream before they came to another. Finally they turned onto the road leading into town. And there at the crossroad, apparently waiting for them, was Booker's brother, John.

"Why, John, what are you doing—" He saw his brother's face and exclaimed, "John! What's the matter?"

Clutching the side of the gig, John told him. Their mother was dead. She had died during the night.

The boy was inconsolable. It was all Reverend Johnson and John could do to get him home. He said it was his fault—that he should have been with her—that she had worked herself to death for him. His grief was wild, primitive, and unreasoning.

Booker did not return to Parkersville. The strike was settled that week—with no increase in pay—and two days after his mother's funeral he went down into the mine. He went over the protests of his stepfather and John.

"Let me alone," he snarled at them. "You think I'm too good to get my face dirty?"

He worked with an energy which astonished other miners, drove through the walls of black slate like a sledge hammer, sent up increasingly large loads of coal. July and most of August went by. Booker lost weight; he snatched at his food like an animal. The foreman raised his pay as a tribute to his driving energy.

Then, four weeks before time for the opening of the term at Hampton, he received a letter from Miss Mackie asking him to return to the Institute two weeks before the opening of school in order that he might assist her in cleaning the buildings and gettings things in order for the new school year.

He held the letter in his grimy hands and read it twice.

Two months before, he had resolved not to return to Hampton at all. He had told John, "Not another cent am I taking from you to go to school!" The hurt look on John's face forced the quivering question from him, "You think I want you to kill yourself—too?" Then, for the first time since their mother's death, the brothers clung together and wept.

But now, as he held Miss Mackie's letter, he had money. And this would give him advanced credit in the treasurer's office. They were all glad when he said he was going back.

In June, 1875, Booker T. Washington graduated from Hampton Institute. He was on the honor roll of commencement speakers.

He had no money, but he had a job. One of the big hotels in Newport, Rhode Island, had offered to take on a number of Hampton students, for the summer, to work as waiters and bus boys. Booker was one of the first to sign up. Rich people had resumed their "summer season" interrupted by the war. During this season, boats ran direct from Norfolk, Virginia, to Newport. And so, immediately after commencement, Booker did go "out to the sea on a big ship."

Newport gave Booker his first glimpse of the North. It was a fascinating new world which lifted from the water in green terraces topped with bare, rocky crags and fringed by broad white beaches. He gazed in wonder at the many-colored pavilions dotting the hillsides where English ivy grew on old stone walls. Here for generations North and South and Europe had come together; the fashionable from all lands strolled along the beaches, frolicked in sheltered caves, and stretched on the white sands. From Newport's wharves, ships had once set sail for China and Liverpool and Africa.

It took Booker some time to become dexterous in table waiting. The gleaming white tables set with fine china, polished silver, and sparkling glasses bewildered him. The guests in raiment he could never have imagined—powdered, perfumed, and always laughing—frightened him. But soon he could swing his tray and flip a napkin with the best of the waiters; before long he began counting his tips, looking forward to his

91

time off, and getting acquainted. He saw more money passing hands than he had ever seen before and the possibility of increasing his earnings was always before him. He was too cautious to gamble, as many of the waiters did; but he stood looking over their shoulders, watching, thinking. He walked along the beach with a pretty little chambermaid. They compared notes as to how they could "make more money." She, too, had people she wanted to help. Booker told her of how little his brother earned working in the mines.

"Now that I've finished school," he said, "I've got to make money!"

Booker marveled at how easy his life was. He tried to push aside painful thoughts. He shrugged his shoulders; bought a pair of white shoes and as the season mounted, bringing with it scores of new guests and increased tips, resolved to enjoy himself—a little.

The first cool winds were sobering. The hotel emptied as guests departed. This "good job" was only for the summer. Now what would he do?

A letter from the Reverend Johnson brought the answer:

Malden is opening a school for its colored children. We presented your name to the School Board. I am happy to tell you that you have been appointed our first teacher. Your salary will be eighteen dollars a month. I know you will come home now.

Two weeks later Booker arrived in Malden.

8

From Malden to the Capital

The schoolhouse was a big converted barn. It had been well built and the workmen who did the remodeling knew they were fixing a place for their own children. They did a good job. All traces of the barn's former occupants had been removed, holes knocked out in the sides to make windows, a floor laid with raised platform in front. Benches and desks from a dismantled school in Charlestown were set in place. There were no blackboards, stands, maps, or books. Such things would have to be assembled by the new teacher.

General Ruffner was a member of the school board. When he expressed himself in favor of Booker's appointment, nobody else was considered. General Ruffner voiced his kinsman's endorsement of Hampton Institute and its methods. Since Dr. William Ruffner was known as Virginia's most distinguished educator, Malden's small board of city fathers preened itself. Their appointee was not only a Hampton graduate but one of their own boys! The colored school, therefore, had an auspicious beginning.

There was, however, a growing element in the border states which viewed the opening of every new school for Negroes with increasing distaste. Negroes, they said—and they used another word—were getting "out of hand." Learning was bad for them—gave them "notions." There was talk of organized efforts to "keep the Negroes in their place."

Unaware of any approaching threat, Booker plunged into what he now considered his life's work. He began by setting the example. With money he brought from Newport he rented a small cottage on the outskirts of town, moved his family, and

93

set Jimmy to clearing the big lot of weeds, brambles, and long-accumulated trash. Early in the morning and late at night he worked on the place—repairing, plastering, painting. Tom had lost his job at the mine the year before. He had been hobbling about town doing odd jobs wherever he could find them. Booker won his stepfather over to the idea of putting in a garden. He demonstrated the use of fertilizer. In a short time the lot beside the cottage was divided into neat patches and rows diligently tended by Tom; a neat picket fence was erected and expertly whitewashed by Jimmy.

Meanwhile good people in the community helped Booker to collect books, slates, pencils, and paper for his school. But, from the beginning, this graduate of Hampton endeavored to do more than teach from the books. His pupils needed everything. Slavery had destroyed the most elemental patterns of living: family life, personal pride, love of home, pride in accomplishment. Booker Washington endeavored to stimulate these attitudes. He taught cleanliness of body and clothing. He distributed and illustrated the use of one small object which caused boundless amusement—a *toothbrush*.

The teacher's sister, Mandy, and Jimmy, whom Jane had "adopted," now attended school every day. It was for John and others like him that Booker started his night school. There were many older boys and girls, as well as men and women, who had to work but longed for some education. From the first his night school was a success. Sometimes the old people's emotions welled out in song. More and more Negroes rode into town from some distance away to "sit in" his school. They were always welcomed. One more could always crowd in.

The younger teacher taught, with only short intervals between sessions, from eight in the morning until ten or eleven at night for five days a week. On Saturdays he visited the homes of his pupils. He did what he could to alleviate conditions which tended to blot out everything the pupil learned at school. Sometimes after such visits Booker returned home discouraged and frustrated, but an hour with Tom in the garden always lifted his spirits. On Sundays he taught a Sunday-school class, after which he spent most of the day reading. He longed for his mother—wished she were with him to see his work—wished she could sit with him in the garden. But now he could think of his mother without bitterness or the gnawing pain of regret. He realized how full her life had been—how richly she had lived—and he promised now to fulfill her every wish for her children.

"You'll be ready for Hampton next fall, John." The two brothers were walking home together after school. The night was fragrant with lilacs, for already it was spring.

"You think so, Booker?"

"Sure! I'll bet they'll give you my old job." Booker punched his elbow into his brother's ribs and added, "Fellow, you'll have to hump yourself!"

"Pshaw, man," boasted John, "they ain't seen nothing yet at Hampton!"

They laughed and agreed that when Booker dismissed his school in June the elder brother would leave the mine in order to devote all his time to study under Booker's supervision.

Teacher, proud parents, and pupils worked together to make the "last day of school" an event. The public was invited and, following the example set at Hampton Institute, the students were given an opportunity to display their newly acquired abilities. In some form or other the teacher saw to it that each one had some part to play. Praise was lavish. The number which perhaps afforded the most enjoyment was little Fannie Smith's rendition of "Thanatopsis." Fannie gestured and rolled her eyes so eloquently that the audience's "Oh's" and "Ah's" spontaneously burst into peals of laughter accompanied by wild applause. Fannie's triumph was so complete that Booker suppressed his impulse to give her a good shaking.

With school out, Booker had more time for what he called his "neighborhood classes." These were not classes at all. He merely went from one house to another suggesting the possibilities of removing rubbish, whitewashing walls, and mending fences. Tom's garden was now a marvel of green abundance. The teacher gave away products from "Pa's garden" and explained how a bushel of beans could be grown in the smallest of areas.

"People all over are talking about our school and our teacher," Preacher Johnson told him, and beamed. "Grannie May insists on reading her Bible aloud to me now. The old lady's been granted her fondest wish—she can read!"

Booker smiled. "Stay and have dinner with us, Reverend," invited Booker. "Afterward I'll walk with you as far as the school."

"What do you have going on there tonight?"

"The old folks wouldn't hear of any summer vacation. I'm afraid my evening classes are not well organized. If the attendance gets much larger we'll have to move out into the field."

"You're liable to bring about a boom in Malden," the Preacher told him. "Better knock out a side of that barn to make room for the folks who are coming!"

"Folks" quite different from what they were expecting called on Booker one night the latter part of August. Tom and the children had gone to bed. Booker and John sat on the porch talking of Hampton. Miss Mackie's letter had come that day— the letter saying she would be willing to "try out" Booker's brother for a job.

"Depend on Miss Mackie to give you a try—but *only* a try!" Booker laughed. "Don't let her stern face frighten you. She's an angel!"

Through the quiet night came the unusual sound of horses' hoofs. The brothers leaned forward listening. The horses were approaching at a rapid pace. They drew nearer—turned into their street. John and Booker could see them in the moonlight as the three horsemen pulled up directly in front of their house!

"Like patrollers!" gasped John, shrinking into the shadow of the porch.

"Patrollers" were night riders, during slavery, who went about terrorizing recalcitrant slaves, searching for runaways, and breaking up gatherings of slaves.

"Sh-sh-sh-sh! Let me handle this," whispered Booker. A cold chill ran down his spine as three booted white men clamped up the walk. He stood up and greeted them.

"Good evening, gentlemen!"

They stopped and stared up at him. The one with a beard

stepped forward and growled, "You the teacher?"

"Yes, sir." Booker spoke pleasantly. "I teach the colored school."

"Come down where we can see you!"

"Won't you all come on the porch and have seats, gentlemen?" asked Booker.

"I said come down here!"

Behind him in the shadows John made a sudden move, and one of the other white men exclaimed, "Who's that?"

"Only my brother, sir."

Booker walked down the steps. Everything about these men was menacing. He knew he was in danger, but his eyes were level and showed no fear. They looked him over as if he were something strange to see.

The second speaker spat on the white picket fence and snarled, "Mighty fine, ain't you, boy—mighty fine!"

The man who apparently was spokesman for the group glared at the speaker, then back at Booker.

"We heared how you're stirring up the black folks around here. And we've come to warn you, just warn you—this time. We don't want your kind here."

"This is my home, sir. I grew up here—I worked in the salt wells and in the mine. I worked in General Ruffner's home. I—"

"Then what you doing so high and mighty now?" the third man interrupted.

"I know," snapped the first spokesman. "You went off to some Yankee school—got your head full of notions. Now you're back to ruin our people."

"I am only teaching them—"

They closed in on him, hemming him in, their evil faces near.

"Stop it! You hear us, boy? Stop it! Go on back to your Yankee friends. You leave our people be. We're telling you. And if you know what's good for your tight hide—you'll listen."

They wheeled about, mounted their horses, and rode away.

Neighbors who had been aroused by their coming, who had

97

peeped through windows and doors, came out. They had not been able to hear what was said, but they knew such late visitors meant no good.

Tom covered his face with shaking hands and moaned, "Dey'll kill yo', boy! Dey'll kill yo'!"

The next day there was excited whispering throughout the town. The horsemen who threatened the teacher were *outsiders*. This fact was declared over and over again. Negroes were somewhat reassured when many white people expressed indignation.

"We're not going to put up with lawlessness in this town," General Ruffner was quoted as saying.

White and Negro schools opened the following Monday. For several nights thereafter Negro men hovered about in the neighborhood and a surprising number of picks, spades, and shovels stood leaning against back doors. The town constable had orders to keep a sharp eye out for strangers hanging about.

Nothing happened and, when John was leaving for Hampton, Booker laughed at the anxious look on his brother's face.

"Stop worrying, John! Those men were simply trying to frighten us. Now that they see we don't scare, they'll leave us alone."

"I wish I could believe that," sighed John.

"Hampton's been threatened, too. Can you imagine General Armstrong running away—or Miss Mackie?"

Booker stood watching the stagecoach as it turned into the road which would take John over the mountains. His eyes misted and he whispered, "He's going back, Ma, not in a broken cart like you rode. He's riding *high*!"

Several prominent people from the surrounding community visited the colored school that fall. They liked what they saw and they complimented the teacher. No doubt it was their favorable comments on the school which deferred further action against it. But just across the border in Ohio an organization which called itself the Ku Klux Klan was gaining prominence. Of this organization Dr. Washington wrote in *Up from Slavery*:

The Ku Klux were bands of men who had joined

themselves together for the purpose of regulating the conduct of colored people, especially with the object of preventing members of the race from exercising any influence in politics . . . but they did not confine themselves to this, because schoolhouses as well as churches were burned by them, and many innocent persons were made to suffer.

The K.K.K. came to Malden on the Friday night before Christmas. They could hardly have known that on this night special "exercises" were being held at the colored school, with the entire School Board invited and General Ruffner himself the chief speaker. Other white visitors sat on the front benches, while behind them were all the Negroes who could crowd into the building. Those who could not get in stood around the door and tried to see and hear through the open windows.

It was a mild night for December. A star-studded sky hung low as the blended voices floated across the fields:

> "Sweet lil' Jesus
> In a lowly manger bo'n,
> Yo' gonna shine, shine, shine
> Lak a lil' sta'!"

Suddenly there was a commotion in the crowd near the door. A boy was pushed through gasping, "Dey's comin'—da pattirollahs! Ah heared 'em in the woods. Dey's comin' tuh burn down da school!"

There was no time for all to get out and get away. Booker ordered his pupils to keep their places. Some of the visitors had come in carriages. The ladies could be hurried away before trouble started. But even while the carriages were being brought up they heard the sound of the pounding hoofs. General Ruffner lifted his voice in stern military fashion, ordering all women and children inside. The men, Negro and white, crowded about the door. They caught up pieces of firewood from the pile stacked in one corner, put out all the lights, and waited.

99

The night riders carried flaming torches. Their hooded figures seemed ghostly and terrifying as they thundered up. They saw the crowd standing in front of the old barn but did not pause. These men were cruel and relentless. The sight of any resistance from black people only infuriated them. *Resistance was brought about by Yankee teaching!* Their leader gave a bloodcurdling yell and the masked men rode into the crowd.

What they met was totally unexpected. Instead of scattering like frightened chickens, the dark mass surged forward and exploded in hard, resounding whacks on horses and riders alike. The Negroes fought to protect their school. The whites fought to protect their honor. Horses reared; blows rained; cries and gasps filled the night. Booker found himself struggling to hold his ground between a whirling Reverend Johnson on one side and a hard-hitting, cursing white man on the other. A whip lashed him across the face—white and black hands dragged riders from their horses before other riders struck them down. Above the din came a hoarse shout from General Ruffner.

"Clement! It's Jeff Clement!"

He had torn the mask from one rider's head. While the rider stared aghast at his father's friend, his horse reared and General Ruffner was thrown to the ground under the hoofs of the maddened animal.

A cry of terror—then a sudden hush fell. The unmasked rider looked about wildly. Then, wheeling his horse, he dashed away. The others followed—trying to shield their faces behind torn robes—their heads lowered, their torches sputtering out on the ground.

General Lewis Ruffner was unconscious when the battered defenders lifted him into his carriage. His wife did not cry as she bent over him. What she had seen that night was no cause for tears. She was proud of her husband.

Booker was blinded by the blood which kept running down from his head as he tried to examine a moaning boy whose leg seemed to be broken. A score of persons were seriously injured. Old folks thanked God that nobody was killed. But

100

some of the younger ones were heard to curse as they staggered down the road with improvised stretchers.

Christmas in Malden that year was not a merry one. Worry and apprehension spread over the town like a pall. Many whites were genuinely shocked that Jeff Clement should have been among the night riders. Others began to ask uneasy questions. *Was a school for Negroes such a good thing?* Sudden silences fell in the homes when dark-skinned servants appeared.

Preacher Johnson was unable to go about his ministerial duties for several weeks. When he did ride out through the county again, he reported signs of trouble everywhere. On one occasion the Preacher was stopped and questioned as to where he was going and why.

Booker heard that a Negro school was burned in Murreysville. His school was running on schedule. Grim lines of determination were forming on the teacher's face. Booker T. Washington was still very young, but already his mantle of responsibility was stained with blood. His stepfather and Mandy now watched anxiously over him. Mandy insisted that she go with him to night school. As soon as they were back they locked and bolted doors and windows. Booker wrote none of this to his brother, John, at Hampton.

Attendance at the school began to fall off. At first it was the children of small farmers in the neighborhood. They tramped miles along the road to school every day. Some layoff on their part was expected during spring planting season, but one boy whispered to the teacher that the "pattirollers" had come to his house. The children were being frightened away from school.

One sunny afternoon Reverend Johnson drove slowly by Booker's home. He pulled up when he saw the teacher working with his father in the garden.

"Hello, there!" he called.

Tom waved his hand and shouted enthusiastically, "Come look at mah new peas, Eldah! Nevah seen nothin' lak 'em in all mah life."

Booker laughed and came forward as the Preacher slowly climbed down from the buggy. "Pa's sure proud of his garden,

101

Reverend," he said. "We'll pick you a sample of these new peas."

"Be right with you, Brother Tom."

Reverend Johnson waved at the gardener, then dropped down on a bench as if too tired to walk farther. He took off his hat and ran his hand over his thin gray hair. Booker thought to himself that his caller had aged recently. He spoke casually.

"Feels like we'll have an early summer. Let me get you a cool drink of water." He started toward the pump.

"Wait, son! I want to talk to you." There was urgency in the voice. Booker returned quickly. But for a minute the bent figure was silent, nervous hands turning the rusty black hat. Then words came, punctuated with painful pauses. "White men stopped me on the road to Parkersville. I told them I was going to preach there Sunday as usual. They turned me back. They would not let me through."

"Things are getting worse, aren't they, Reverend?" said Booker quietly.

Something like a groan came from the man on the bench. "I'm getting too old to go through it all again; I thought we were out of bondage—free to move forward." He shook his head. "I came here from Canada, where my father took me when I was very small. I went to school there. But God sent me back—back here to labor among His most lowly, most sorely oppressed people. I've tried to be faithful to Him—but now I'm getting old—and the road is still so long—so rocky— so steep. I haven't the strength—any more." The gray head sank lower.

Booker laid his hand on the shaking shoulder and pressed hard.

"Nonsense, Reverend, you're strong in goodness and faith. The people know that you—" His voice choked as the dark face lifted to his.

"God needs young men in His vineyard now, son. Young men like you." Booker started. Reverend Johnson looked away, his voice calmer. "Ever since that Sunday you spoke in church —that Sunday when the light of heaven shone from your dear mother's face—I've thought that God has called you to preach.

I don't want to press you, Booker—but time is running out—for me. We need help—more help."

"My school—what about my school?" A note of desperation sounded in the young man's voice.

"You've done wonders here with your teaching." He laid his hand on Booker's arm. "But I don't think the School Board's going to open our school next fall."

"What? What do you say, sir?"

"Mr. Standish told me they think it might be just as well to close the school—until things settle down."

Booker was thoughtfully silent for the next few days. Does a man change his life's work? He was a *teacher*. He had never been so happy. He could look around and see what he was accomplishing. Yet, unmistakably, things were getting worse—not better—for Negroes throughout the Southland. This was the spring of 1877, when hopes for a genuine reconstruction had perished; lawlessness prevailed and organized efforts for advancement were being strangled.

The last day of school was not a festive occasion. Everybody knew by then that the school would not reopen in the fall. The teacher was being "let out" along with his pupils. There was plenty of brave talk about "when school opened," but hearts were heavy that day. Yet only in Booker's mind was there any doubt about his own future. Everybody else was certain that "Sistah Washin'ton's boy" had been "called to preach."

All through slavery the plantation Preacher had been the wisest, least shackled, and most valiant man among the slaves. He had been "called by God" and therefore endowed with special gifts of insight and power. Even the masters frequently exempted him from demands made on other slaves. Masters recognized him as a relic of faraway tribal life who could prove valuable in keeping the slaves together and adjusting them to new conditions. To a people struggling toward freedom "the Preacher" became natural leader and guide. He was looked up to and obeyed, given the best of whatever little they had, honored in every way possible.

It is not surprising that, when they first learned to read and write, many Negroes received a "call to preach." This "call" was described as an awesome experience. Usually it came when the individual was sitting in church. Without warning the one called would fall on the floor, perhaps lie there speechless and motionless for hours. Such a call could not be ignored.

Booker Washington told Reverend Johnson and others who continued to make plans for him that he had no "call."

"Surely," he said, "if I am called to preach I would know it."

"You're trying too hard, son," remonstrated Reverend Johnson. "You're too busy. You can't hear the still, small voice. You need time for thought and prayerful study." His face lit up with a smile.—*"I've got it!* The Baptists have opened a seminary for Negroes in Washington, D. C. Let me write the Board about you! I know they'd make it possible for you to attend."

Booker gave his consent and the letter went off immediately. Within two weeks they had an answer. The Baptist Board had considered the application of Mr. Booker T. Washington for admission to Wayland Seminary. In view of the fact that Mr. Washington was a graduate of Hampton Institute, had for two years taught in the public schools of Malden, and was so highly recommended by his pastor, the Baptist Mission Board would pay his tuition at Wayland Seminary, where he would be admitted as a student. Room and board could be had at a nominal cost either at the school or with some Christian family in Washington. Reverend Johnson was elated. Booker wrote his brother, John, who with other Hampton students was starting a season of work at Narragansett Pier.

Summer resorts had been pleased with the experiment of hiring Hampton students. They learned their jobs quickly, were clean and courteous. John had the choice of several big hotels for his summer "vacation." Upon receipt of Booker's letter suggesting that he might enter Wayland Seminary in the fall, John wrote urging Booker to join him at the summer resort.

"There's a job here waiting for you and you'll need money in Washington. We can both make more money waiting table than doing anything else."

Booker knew that John was right. So once more he donned

a white jacket, flipped a napkin, and reached for tips from the rich and idle.

The season at Narragansett Pier was a gay and profitable one. This was the summer of 1878. Northern industrialists congratulated themselves and the administration that the "reconstruction period" was over. Discord between the states was a thing of the past. President Hayes recalled all troops from the South; federal assistance to ex-slaves was discontinued. They were told that they could go to work.

If the state of the country could be judged by the lavish prosperity of the summer colonies around Narragansett Bay, everything was fine. Booker sent money home, yet he felt like a rich man the September morning he stepped down from the train in Washington, D. C., and stared up at the gleaming white dome of the Capitol. Carrying his suitcase, he walked slowly in the direction of the dome. His first sight of the capitol city thrilled him. For two hours he wandered about the wide, shaded avenues, gazed at government buildings, and stood close beside the iron fence surrounding the White House. *What a beautiful city!* he thought over and over again.

At last he took out his letter, asked directions, and within a short time presented himself at Wayland Seminary to begin a course of study for the ministry.

◇◇◇◇◇◇◇◇◇◇◇◇◇◇◇◇◇◇◇ **9** ◇◇◇◇◇◇◇◇◇◇◇◇◇◇◇◇◇◇◇

More Knowledge and a Goal

Latin and Greek cast a shadow over Booker Washington's life from the day he entered Wayland Seminary. Hampton Institute included neither in its curriculum, so the young man was totally unprepared for his sudden immersion in the classics. The bearded theologians who guided the seminary recognized no necessity for relating their subjects to the background, understanding, or needs of their students. These Doctors of Divinity would have considered themselves sorely remiss had they failed to teach their darker brothers to rattle off *amo, amas, amat* and to recognize the several declensions of Greek nouns. Booker was dumfounded to hear a pupil praised for deciphering a line of Latin into English every word of which needed correcting.

At Hampton, Booker had often joined excited groups to discuss how some recently acquired knowledge could be applied at home. Now he asked himself how and where he was going to use Latin or Greek. He was baffled by the students' frequently expressed enthusiasm for learning these languages. One loud-mouthed, coarse fellow in his Latin class particularly exasperated him.

Finally the Hampton graduate asked, "Bates, what are you going to *do* with Latin?"

The student turned a pudgy round face and his eyes were wide with amazement.

"What d' yo' mean—*do* with hit?" he asked. He drew nearer and declared, "Ah'm gettin' eddicated so Ah won't have to do nothin'—long as Ah lives!"

Fortunately not all the students at Wayland Seminary were motivated by the same purpose. Booker was drawn to a number of earnest men who also boarded in the school. They had been sent by the Baptist Board from widely scattered areas and were planning to go back and serve their people. Some had jobs on the outside; all had to live on the bare edge of necessity. Two of these men were so poorly trained in the basic elements of reading and writing that Booker took it upon himself to aid them. He formed a "study class," so they spent their evenings together. And these older men taught Booker. From them he heard what Negroes were doing in Georgia, Florida, the Carolinas, and Mississippi.

One evening someone mentioned the "great Frederick Douglass" and they told him, "There's nobody in the world like Frederick Douglass! He makes you proud! You'll get a chance to hear him!"

Such talk made Booker glad he had come to Washington—in spite of Latin and Greek.

There were those at Wayland who far surpassed Booker. Most of them were day students who wore good clothes, carried themselves with assurance, and gave evidence of being well supplied with money. They arrived barely in time for classes and when dismissed they hurried off to more enjoyable pursuits.

These young men scarcely glanced at the big, serious-faced teacher from West Virginia until the morning David Smalls turned and said affably, "I hear you're from Hampton, Washington. I'm interested in that school. How about me picking you up one afternoon? I'd like to hear about it."

Booker readily agreed. The next day was Saturday, with no classes. Smalls promised, "I'll come by about two o'clock. Show you a bit of Washington."

He looked forward to a pleasant walk with someone who knew the city well, but he did not expect the smart little buggy in which Smalls drove up to the school the following afternoon. The autumn day was clear and bright—perfect for a drive.

"I'll show you the sights," said Smalls as they turned into Pennsylvania Avenue, "then we'll drive out to Howard University and talk about schools."

"Howard University?" questioned Booker.

"That's the really big school in the suburbs. They have both Negro and white students." The driver flipped his whip gracefully. "I'm thinking of going out there myself next year. I want to study medicine."

The careless indifference with which the young man uttered these statements sounded reprehensible to Booker. He set his lips in a stern line and stared straight ahead, hardly hearing the well-bred, modulated voice at his side. Where had this Negro been all his life that he could speak so lightly of "studying medicine"?

But that night, as he lay on his cot in Wayland Seminary, Booker searched his mind for the word to describe David Smalls. It came unexpectedly and Booker smiled in the darkness. Obviously one who had spent the first years of his life in slavery on Burroughs Plantation had to adjust his own thinking before applying a *white* expression to a man of his own color. "Gentleman" was the word for David Smalls. This young Negro from South Carolina was a *gentleman*.

A real friendship developed between these two whose lives up to that time would hardly have differed more had one been born white and the other black. With Smalls to coach him, irregular verbs, declensions, and hieroglyphyics no longer haunted Booker's dreams. His natural aptitude for public speech was released. He made other friends. And through these new friends Booker Washington caught sight of another world of Negroes—a world he was never wholly to comprehend and in which he would always be uncomfortable.

It is unfortunate that his own contacts were only with the outer, frazzled fringe of this world. He did not think much of the well-dressed sons and daughters at Howard University whose object in life seemed to be a "good time," nor of the government clerks who were always in debt or the girls who preened themselves in expensive dresses while their mothers bent over washtubs. He saw the spendthrifts and imitators. But behind these was a substantial community, neither black nor white, proud and capable, whose strength was demonstrated by individual achievements but whose weakness lay in its lack of cohesion.

Several families of free Negroes had settled in Washington, D. C., when Thomas Jefferson was President. Through the years this group had been increased, sometimes by Negroes who bought their freedom, sometimes by the sons and daughters of masters who had declared them free. The latter were frequently left property in Washington or Baltimore in their fathers' wills. In time there developed in Washington, in nearby Baltimore, and in such cities as Charlestown, South Carolina, an "upper class" of colored people who were neither poverty-stricken nor uneducated. Washingtonians were prevented from entering politics, but in 1866, when citizenship and civil rights were granted to Negroes, these communities had begun to exert powerful political influence.

When Booker Washington met David Smalls, his uncle,

Robert Smalls, had already served one term in the House of Representatives as member from his state of South Carolina. Four other Negroes were in Congress that winter of 1878-79. One of them was Senator B. K. Bruce from Mississippi. But the man—white or black—in public life probably most talked about that year was Frederick Douglass. President Rutherford B. Hayes had just appointed him United States Marshal of the District of Columbia. Never before in the history of the United States had a Negro filled such a post. This was not only a judicial position of importance but one which required Douglass' attendance at all formal state functions.

"Oh," exclaimed Booker Washington, "if I could only be a fly on the wall! If I could only see with my own eyes this man who was once a slave standing beside the President of the United States!" He closed his eyes in ecstatic contemplation.

David Smalls laughed. "I doubt if even Senator Bruce could change you into a fly, but he might be able sometime to get us tickets which would admit us to the White House."

"No!" shouted Booker in disbelief.

"Yes!" came back Smalls.

About a week before the Christmas holiday Smalls caught up with Booker in the hall and whispered, "Come over after supper! We've got a problem."

That evening when Booker arrived at the house where Smalls lived he discovered two other acquaintances closeted with Smalls in his room. The three regarded him seriously— their eyes measuring him from head to foot. A chill of apprehension swept over young Washington.

He asked, "What's the matter here? What's happened?"

One of the young men shook his head solemnly.

"I doubt we can do it, Smalls. His shoulders are too broad. And what a big head!"

Booker's face made them burst into laughter. Then they told him. Smalls had tickets for the President's Thursday-evening reception. Frederick Douglass would be in his place. There was, however, one small fly in the ointment: formal attire was required.

Booker's soaring spirits collapsed. He shook his head.

109

"That settles it for me." He tried to sound indifferent.

"Don't take defeat so easily, my friend," Smalls chided him. "Now then, fellows, let's see what we can do."

Four young men contributed to Booker Washington's wardrobe for the important occasion. Smalls insisted that he come to his house to dress.

"This is my party," he said, "and it must be right."

On Thursday evening when Booker surveyed himself in a long mirror he could only stare. Nobody in Malden would have recognized him.

"Really quite handsome, Washington," murmured Smalls. "You do make a very personable figure." He took one quick look at himself in the mirror. "Well, pull on your gloves and let's be going!"

Booker was certain they would be stopped at the White House gates. He was sure the stiff hat would tumble off his head as he mounted the White House steps. Instead the personage at the door merely glanced at the two cards in Smalls' hand, a functionary took the hat from his shaking hand, and the former coal miner found himself entering a lofty room filled with people whose splendor frightened him. He feared that his mere presence would affront them.

As a matter of fact, this was a thoroughly democratic gathering. President and Mrs. Hayes were receiving members of Congress, their friends and constituents as a kind of preholiday good-will gesture. The appearance of two genteel young colored men did not cause a commotion. Congressman Smalls saw them at once and came forward.

"Ah, here you are, David!" he said. "And this is your friend from West Virginia. I've been waiting for you."

Booker shook hands with the Congressman and murmured politely, but he scarcely knew what he was doing. He had recognized Frederick Douglass immediately. The great head with its bushy mane sweeping back from wide forehead, its deep-set eyes and jutting bull-bearded jaw, was set on massive shoulders that lifted it above the crowd. *What a man!* thought Booker as Congressman Smalls propelled him into the long line that was slowly moving toward the front of the parlor. From the next room came the music of a string quartet which mingled pleasantly with the murmur of many voices, light laughter, and the tinkle of glasses.

Then he was opposite the imposing figure. He felt the keen eyes searching his face; he heard Congressman Smalls saying, "Allow me to present Booker Washington, Mr. Douglass. He is a graduate of Hampton Institute and a student at Wayland Seminary."

"I am happy to meet you, Mr. Washington. Young men ike you are an honor to our race." The golden voice wrapped itself around his heart as the big hand held his in a warm clasp.

Then the United States Marshal turned to the straight, austere figure at his side and said, "Mr. President—with your permission—Mr. Washington."

And Booker Washington shook hands with the President of the United States!

The evening was like a dream to the boy from Malden. On their way out he was introduced to Senator Bruce and his statuesque, honey-colored wife. Booker had never seen such a beautiful woman.

The two young men walked home through the crisp December night. Booker's voice rang with conviction as he exclaimed, "Now I *know* what I want!"

Smalls smiled tolerantly. "And what is that?" he asked.

"I want to be like Frederick Douglass!"

The other lifted his eyebrows. "The Honorable Frederick Douglass is the greatest man our race has produced. You've picked out quite a job for yourself, chum."

Meanwhile Negroes in Malden were putting up a fight for their school. Reverend Johnson; Nat Calvert, livery-stable owner; George Peters, the carpenter, and Matt Smith, Fannie Smith's father, traveled all the way to Wheeling to lay their case before the state legislature. They tried to persuade Barber Wells to go along with them, but he was afraid such a thing would offend his customers. The barber was probably right. As a result of the appearance in the state capital of Negroes from Malden, people all over the state began talking about the

111

colored school at Malden. And wherever they talked about the school they talked about its teacher—Booker Washington.

There were not as many black people in West Virginia as in the states which were sending Negro Congressmen to Washington, but with the agitation over schools for their children went the reminder that *Negroes could now vote.* The thing the K.K.K. had been organized to prevent was happening: Negroes were turning to politics.

A harassed legislator hastened to Malden. Shortly afterward word was circulated that the "colored school in Malden would be resumed in the fall." Negroes, however, continued to talk about voting.

Charleston was entertaining political ambitions that spring. Its businessmen saw great advantage in Charleston's becoming capital of the state. For some time there had been considerable discussion throughout West Virginia over the question of moving the capital of the state from Wheeling to some more central point. The new legislature designated three cities to be voted upon as the permanent seat of government. They were Wheeling, Charleston, and Huntington. Wheeling had the advantage of being in possession of the coveted seat. It was large and its location on the Ohio River guaranteed its importance. Huntington was also on the Ohio River, had the advantage of facing the rapidly expanding West, and was easily accessible. But Charleston was in the very center of powerful mining interests. Politicians determined on a piece of strategy that would harness the state's large, new Negro vote to its band wagon.

Early in March, Booker Washington, at Wayland Seminary, received a letter from a committee of prominent white citizens in Charleston inviting him to canvass the state in the interest of making "your neighboring city the capital of our fine state." The sum of money mentioned in the letter made Booker's eyes pop. Life was so full of surprises that the young man did not puzzle his brain over why such an offer should be made to him. He was full of confidence in these days. He was looking for opportunities. And one question was quite settled in his own mind: *he was not called to preach.* He answered the letter without delay, saying he would be in Charleston by the tenth of March.

A few days before leaving Washington, Booker had the opportunity of hearing Frederick Douglass speak at Howard University, of which Mr. Douglass was a trustee. Douglass' forceful presentation of facts, the strength of his arguments, his eloquence, and his direct simplicity moved Booker as no man's words had ever done before. One little story so impressed the young man that years later he related it in his *Up from Slavery*. Mr. Douglass told how once when he was traveling in the state of Pennsylvania he was forced, because of his color, to ride in the baggage car. A number of indignant white passengers went forward to offer their sympathy. One of them said, "I'm sorry, Mr. Douglass, that you have been degraded in this manner." Douglass' reply to this was, "They cannot degrade Frederick Douglass. The soul that is within me no man can degrade. I am not the one that is being degraded on account of this treatment, but those who are inflicting it upon me."

Booker's seven months in Washington had been rich in friendships and experiences, but nothing was to prove so valuable to him as he moved one step nearer his life's work than these simple words of Frederick Douglass.

The Charleston Committee launched its campaign carefully. Booker Washington was first presented in the churches of that city. He was preceded by a member of the Committee who told the audience how fortunate it was to have as its speaker tonight "one of our own boys, a graduate of Hampton Normal and Agricultural Institute, a student of theology at Wayland Seminary in Washington, D. C., and a teacher in the public schools of our neighboring thriving town, Malden."

This introduction brought brisk applause from Negro and white audiences alike. Whatever nervousness Booker might have felt was quickly dispelled by the friendly faces. The issue with which he dealt was not one calling for condemnation or bitter recriminations. At a time when most questions had to do with the struggle between apprehensive whites and the newly declared black citizens, this discussion of "where our state capital should be located" was one which brought these two elements together in a common interest. Negroes were proud and delighted that a member of their race had been chosen to present the important issue throughout the state; whites

113

became increasingly interested in the young Negro who could speak without bluster on a subject which concerned them. Young Washington's calm bearing, his easy speech touched with quaint humor, his respect for all opponents won for him immense popularity throughout the state.

The campaign lasted three months. When the vote was taken in June, Charleston won the distinction of becoming capital of West Virginia.

The young orator returned home to Malden to find a letter awaiting him from General Armstrong inviting him to deliver the postgraduate address at Hampton for the approaching commencement.

Flushed with victory and with the plaudits of both races ringing in his ears, Booker returned to his *alma mater*. Trains now rolled out of Malden over the newly constructed railroad. He bought his ticket and traveled in style along the route he had pursued only a few years before. Now he stared out the window and considered a dazzling future. The train wheels clicked out a refrain: *We'll send you to Congress!*

It is quite possible that had Booker Washington not made this trip at this time he would have succumbed to pressing demands that he go into politics. There were many incentives. The young man had just cast his first vote. He had felt his own power as audiences swayed toward him, hanging on his words. He had savored the burst of applause which sometimes mounted to an ovation. He had seen the rich rewards gleaned by the successful politician. He imagined himself back in Washington, wearing a silk hat, riding in a carriage.

Three days at Hampton made as deep an impression on him as the former graduate did on his teachers, an admiring student body, and the host of relatives, friends, trustees, and sponsors who gathered at Hampton Institute for its tenth commencement.

Virginia Hall was completed. It stood proud and stately on the gently sloping grounds overlooking the sparkling little bay. Gone were the unsightly old tents and in their place were graveled walks, green grass, and plots glowing with many-colored flowers. The students seemed younger and more alert

114

than those of his day. They were just as busy. And the teachers were just the same—straight and slender and anxious, and always busy.

Booker sat alone in John's room and smiled as the familiar sounds of preparation for the "last day" drifted in through the open window: chorus practice in the music room, hammering, pounding, running footsteps on the gravel walk, voices calling out, laughter in the June night. On this night "lights out" bell was delayed. Nobody wanted to go to bed. It would be some time before John came in. Booker took off his coat, adjusted the lamp on the small table, and bent over his speech for the morrow.

Hampton had never had such a large turnout for its commencement exercises. The chorus sang as if inspired. Booker Washington was greeted with applause when he rose to speak. His subject was "The Force That Wins." It was a youthful speech prepared with all the courage and assurance of the very young. It was wide-flung and visionary, but gradually another quality came through—a faith secured by suffering and pain, compassion and forgiveness for the weak, a promise and hope for the defeated. The young man on the platform was speaking from some age-old, inner knowledge; some strength absorbed from his mother, something she had had from generations of women who had borne their sons in suffering and great sorrow. And, as he spoke, the audience suddenly saw him as a symbol of a people rising out of slavery to fulfill the promises of ages. He was that new being among the peoples of the world: the American Negro, poised, eager, unafraid, on the threshold of life.

There was complete silence when the vibrant voice stopped and the speaker turned back to his seat. Not until he covered his face with a shaking hand did the storm break. Then applause came in tumultuous waves which only mounted with the passing moments. Someone plucked at Booker's sleeve. "Stand up! Stand up and bow!" He rose to his feet and many in the audience rose with him. He saw Miss Mackie dabbing her eyes with the ever-present cambric handkerchief; he saw Mr. Larry's flushed face as he clapped his hands; he saw all their shining eyes. He saw smiles on the stiff New England faces and a warm glow filled his heart.

As the ripples of applause subsided, the principal of Hampton came forward. He stood silent until a hush fell over the hall, then bowed his head and in a voice choked with emotion implored God's choicest blessings on this "young man who found his way to us only a few short years ago, who has now gone forth to serve his people as a shining example of Thy good and bountiful mercies. We thank Thee that we have had some small share in preparing him for service. Bless and keep him always in the path of righteousness, goodness, and mercy." From all over the hall came the fervent echoes of General Armstrong's "Amen." Tears started from Booker's eyes. He felt humble and ashamed of the little he had done. He slipped out of the hall by the back way and could not be found when the exercises were over.

Later that afternoon he kept an appointment in General Armstrong's office. The young man was surprised at the amount of information the General had about him. To questions he replied, "No, sir, I am not going into the ministry," and "Yes, sir, I'm returning to Malden to resume work in the school there."

"Keep in touch with me, Washington. Dr. Ruffner gives us a most favorable report of what you have done in Malden." He extended his hand. "Hampton is proud of you!"

Booker persuaded John to accompany him home.

"We can afford the trip," he said, "and a little rest won't hurt you. Besides," he added, "Pa's getting quite feeble. Mandy and Jim are growing like young colts. I'm anxious to get them back in school."

So, for the last time, the little family was all together that summer. Jane, their mother, was with them perhaps more fully than she had ever been in the flesh. As Tom looked at her two fine sons, as he listened to their talk and watched their comings and goings, he talked constantly of their mother. When Booker told his sister, "You're getting to look like Ma, Mandy," the girl's sober face lighted with a smile and she tried harder than ever to be like Jane.

Everybody was glad to see the teacher back. Reverend Johnson's nearsighted eyes grew wistful, but he had to acknowledge that if Booker did not yet feel the "call" he must not be forced. The School Board was quite willing to open the school for evening classes before fall if the reemployed teacher so desired. His salary had been raised to twenty-five dollars, but it would not start until September.

After two weeks John went off to his job at Narragansett Pier. Booker yielded to the pleas all about him and began setting up his evening classes. He declined invitations from half a dozen places to come and speak.

Tom "took to his bed" the middle of July. He had been a strong, sturdy man when he had his accident in the coal mine seven years before. Now he was an old man. His last years had been easy and without want. He told visiting neighbors how good Jane's boys had been to him; he told Mandy she need not be afraid, her brothers would take care of her; he told Jimmy to grow up to be like Jane's boys—and then he died peacefully.

They buried the only father they had ever known in the little graveyard beside his wife. They knew he would rest easy there.

As if to allow no time for grief, a letter came from General Armstrong containing an amazing offer:

> We should like to invite you to come to Hampton to pursue supplementary studies and to assist us with an experimental matter which we have undertaken for the U. S. Government. Last spring a request came to us from Captain R. H. Pratt at Fort Marian, Florida, to permit him to bring to Hampton a number of Indians who for three years had been imprisoned at Fort Marian. Captain Pratt had undertaken to tame these wild men and had been so successful that at the end of their prison terms twenty-two of the younger men begged to learn more of the white man's ways instead of being sent immediately to the Indian reservation. Captain Pratt considered Hampton the best place where they might receive some training in industry and self-help as well as in English.

117

We granted Captain Pratt's request. He brought his Indians and camped with them on our grounds. Their response was so favorable that Captain Pratt called the matter to the attention of Mr. Carl Schurz, Secretary of the Interior. The Secretary of War and the Commissioner on Indian Affairs have now agreed to the education of Indians at Hampton Institute and have set aside a sum of money for this purpose. We shall be expecting a large party of Indians from the Dakotas this fall. We feel that you are well equipped to assist us in civilizing these young red men. I need not say that . . .

"Indians!" gasped Mandy, interrupting further reading of the letter.

It was incredible, yet there it was in General Armstrong's own precise, clear handwriting. The General was asking him to return to Hampton to teach Indians! Booker was torn between delight and despair. The prospect of going back to Hampton to be part of the great work being done there was wonderful—to be asked to assist in an extraordinary and unusual experiment was indeed an honor. On the other hand, what about all his carefully laid plans for the school in Malden? Eager pupils were waiting. The town, indeed an entire state, was expecting him to do great things. People in West Virginia would think him crazy to go back to Hampton to teach *Indians*!

In the next several weeks a number of letters passed between Hampton and Malden. Hampton endeavored to solve Booker's two major problems: a Hampton graduate was located who said he would be glad to teach Malden's school; Booker's sister, Amanda, and his young brother, James, would be admitted as students at Hampton.

Mandy walked with him to the post office the afternoon Booker sent off his final letter of acceptance. As they turned out of the Square on the way home, a brown dimpled girl in a flowered dress almost ran into them.

"Hello, Fannie," exclaimed Booker's sister. "Where you going in such a hurry?"

The girl stopped, looking down as if embarrassed. Booker

saw the sweep of her long black eyelashes and the silken ripple in the puff of her hair.

"Just passin' by, Mandy, honey," she said in a low, melodious voice. Then her whole face lighted; she flashed a dazzling smile upward with the words, "Howdy, Mister Teacher. We all so glad 'bout school!"

Before he could catch his breath she had gone tripping down the street, her flowered dress fluttering.

Booker swallowed. "Well," he blurted, "who's your pretty friend, Mandy?"

Mandy stared at her brother in amazement. "You don't remember Fannie Smith?"

"Fannie Smith. That can't be—" That skinny little monkey who had almost ruined his program with her "Thanatopsis"! Oh, no!

Mandy giggled. "It sure is. And will Miss Fannie be sick when she hears we're going away. She's crazy about you!"

"Mandy!" Elder brother appeared to be properly shocked. But behind the annoyed frown the young man was wondering whether it was not his duty to look up his willful pupil, Fannie Smith, before leaving Malden.

10

"Come Down and Help Us"

They were a sorry lot—the Indians who had just been brought in from North Dakota. They squatted on the floor or stood leaning against the walls of the big hall clutching faded old blankets tight about their thin bodies in spite of the warm day. Disheveled locks hung halfway to their knees or were braided with strips of red flannel down each side of sullen, scarred faces. They had traveled a thousand miles in army wagons accompanied by armed soldiers. All along the way people had stared and jeered and pointed fingers at them. They had no clothes into which to change, no water with which to wash. Gone were their chiefs, their heroes, all their stalwart braves—all fallen as they fought to defend homes, children, and the graves of their ancestors. Gone were the forests, the buffaloes, the lakes and rivers. Only they were left—these wards of the white men who had taken everything.

Booker Washington stood beside the door and looked at them. He was stunned by what he saw. All that he knew about Indians was that they were "savages" who tried to block "progress." They had once roved all over America scalping one another, filling the night with their war cries, and engaging in all sorts of "heathenish" practices. The white man had tried to civilize them, but they were too lazy to work. Now these red men were being shown mercy by a benevolent government which had appropriated one hundred and sixty-seven dollars apiece for their education. They were going to be given all the blessings of civilization and Christianity. They ought to be deeply grateful. Yet there was no gratitude in the eyes which slowly lifted to his. Silently, motionless, with wooden faces, they stared at him. Whatever it was in their eyes made him extremely uncomfortable. Yet he had to do something. He was in charge and this was Hampton Institute. He stiffened and spoke sternly.

"Stand up—all of you!"

Nobody moved. The stillness was broken by a hacking cough. He did not turn his head, but suddenly out of the depths of his being came that wave of sympathetic awareness which was to illumine Washington's decisions: *these Indians needed food, not discipline.* His face broke into a smile.

"You probably don't understand a word I'm saying"—he let his smile encompass them all—"but you just rest here until I see about getting you some food. You must be very tired." He extended his hand in an intuitive gesture, then turned and disappeared through the open door.

It was at least three hours before suppertime and Washington knew the cook would probably be alone in the big bare kitchen which always smelled of lye and onions. Mrs. Green was formidable enough when surrounded by her phalanx of student help. The consequences to anyone who invaded her kitchen at this quiet hour might be dire. The young man trembled, but he persevered.

"Mrs. Green," he asked meekly, "could I have some food for the Indians now?"

"Now?" The cook reared back indignantly.

"Yes, ma'am—now."

In the end Washington's persuasive charm prevailed. Nothing like it had happened at Hampton before. The huge iron pots which were simmering on the stoves were pulled forward; forty heavy bowls were taken down from the shelves; two passing students were pressed into service and the food brigade was organized. Within the hour he was back in the big hall carrying a huge basket with the bowls, spoons, and bread—while behind him came the boys, each bringing a pail of thick, savory stew.

Though the Indians appeared to be exactly as he had left them, their apparent apathy concealed a lively interest in the man who stood at the door and spoke to them of friendship and good will. For this is what the outstretched hand had said to them. They had not understood the words—but they had seen the smile on his face; they had seen the hand with its lifted palm. What did this mean?

"He no white man," spoke one in the ancient language of the Sioux.

"He no black," pointed out another.

White men they knew too well; some of them had seen black slaves. The first they feared; the second they despised. But what was this one whose skin was neither white nor black—this one who said he was their friend?

And now he brought them good warm food! They accepted the bowls from his hand with words which in their language meant "Thank you." He heard what sounded to him like grunts, but he saw their eyes and nodded his head. The two boys who had carried the pails watched the strange wild men whose arrival had caused so much excitement throughout the school.

"They's starving," whispered one.

A start had been made, but before these newcomers could take their place in the institution whose purpose was "to inculcate industrious habits, order and good conduct in every respect" much more had to be done. These forty were only the first lot of Indians who would occupy a whole building set aside for them. Neat army cots, tables, and stools were waiting. Miss Mackie had sent over two barrels of mission clothing. The Indians would have to discard their filthy rags, wash themselves thoroughly, and put on decent clothes.

Had it occurred to the instructor to lead his wards the short distance down the slope to the bay and indicate that they might plunge into the water, the matter of bathing would have been much more easily resolved. In their natural habitat the Sioux kept their bodies scrupulously clean. But bathing in the waters about Hampton was as foreign to peoples of that region as were the great wooden tubs of lye suds to the red men of Dakota. Confronted with these tubs, they clung to their rags, shuddered, and backed away in terror. Not until Booker stripped himself and stepped into one would anybody come near them. Then they slowly gathered round; one Indian put out his hand and ran his fingers along the bare, muscular arm which did not flinch or pull away.

He turned to the others and announced approvingly, "Good! This one built like big chief. He strong!" And, letting his blanket fall, he shook off his moccasins, unfastened filthy leggings, and followed the "chief's" example.

They all took their turns and afterward there were grunts of dismay and some giggles when the mission clothes were brought out. Their soiled, faded blankets had been woven with loving care. The signs of their totems and clans still showed among the dirty tatters. The Sioux watched with heavy hearts as their last possessions were kicked into a corner.

Not, however, until it became evident that they would have to part with their long hair did open rebellion threaten. Then they jabbered, waved their hands, and backed away from the barber.

"What I'm gonna do?" he asked. "These Injines is crazy!"

122

"We'll have to get help!" came the determined answer. "Their hair must be cut."

Years later Washington realized what ignominy his actions heaped upon the young red men that day. One slender, frail boy backed into a corner and covered his face with his hands. His grandfather had been a great chief of the Sioux. The boy's long hair was his only relic of past glory. As his shoulders heaved, a hard hand gripped his elbow, nails dug into his quivering flesh, and harsh syllables sounded close to his ear.

"Stop it! You disgrace our ancestors by crying like a woman! They watch us now." The older Indian relaxed his grip on the trembling arm. His voice sank. "Remember!" he said, and the Sioux word was like the winds blowing across the open plains. "Remember they will come back. Our braves will rise from their graves and avenge us. Courage, brother!"

Late this night when Washington made his final round of inspection he could not know that every one of the Indians who lay so straight and still on the army cot was awake, that forty pairs of lips whispered into the darkness. The young Sioux called upon their great departed ones to look down from their Happy Hunting Grounds and see them, shorn and defenseless. And they asked for patience and courage until the great ones returned.

The first few weeks were difficult, but gradually a system of communication was established. Washington repeated his words over and over, accompanying them with actions, until little by little they were understood. The Indians trusted him and responded to his orders. Students, on the whole, were sympathetic and helpful, though since Indians were not admitted to any white school some felt that they should not be admitted to Hampton. But, as they acquired English, the Indians gradually glided into study with the others. When fresh lots arrived they were guided by the more experienced. A family life was developed and Washington found himself living in the big house with seventy-five Indian youths. They called him "Chief" and regarded him as such. To the rest of the school, he was "house father" to the Indians. The building where they lived together was called "Wigwam."

123

President Hayes cited the new enterprise in his December message to Congress, saying, "I agree with the Secretary of the Interior that the result of this interesting experiment, if favorable, may be destined to become an important factor in the advancement of civilization among the Indians."

As the last day of school approached, it became obvious that the "house father" would have to remain at Hampton with his Indians during the summer. John was graduating that June and Booker was rather looking forward to returning to Malden. He still thought of the Malden school as "my school." He wanted to see what his colleague had accomplished. In fact, he had unfinished business in Malden. He wondered if Fannie Smith was less "frivolous."

After his graduation John was immediately assigned to a job in Hampton's rapidly expanding shop. The job would not start until September, so he went off once more to Narragansett Pier. Mandy also was going somewhere. Mrs. Courtley Palmer, wealthy sponsor of Hampton, had written Miss Mackie asking if she had a student who could assist with her two children for the summer. "You know the kind of girl I should want, my dear Miss Mackie," she wrote. Miss Mackie did know. She sent off her reply recommending Miss Amanda Washington as being "genteel, capable and completely dependable." On the last day of school an excited Miss Mandy left for Philadelphia.

When the last school cart rolled away, Booker and Jimmy were left behind. Remembering his own melancholy when the school emptied, Booker moved young Jimmy into "Wigwam" with him. This proved to be a happy solution for everyone concerned. The boy was taken more closely into the Indians' confidence than the "Chief," who, after all, represented authority. James discovered the Indians' longing to go out on the shimmering waters. In no time at all they built a boat which they took turns using. The instructor saw how their spirits were lifted and with what renewed zest they tackled their work.

The summer crawled by—pleasantly enough, but for the first time in his life Booker was acutely conscious of loneliness. He wished he were with his brother at Narragansett Pier. John had time off from work—and there were girls!

General Samuel Armstrong did not take a vacation that summer, either. The heart-rending efforts of a whole people wanting to learn filled him with the determination to open more and more channels to them. Hampton Institute was growing. Several rich endowments had made possible new buildings, new shops, and more equipment for the farm. But much more was needed. There were always more students than there was room. There were scores of men and women, earnestly desiring an education, who were too poor to pay any portion of the cost of their board or to supply themselves with books. Hundreds of begging letters went out urging rich patrons to "educate a worthy young Negro" by supplying the money to meet these needs, but still there was not enough.

That summer the principal decided to start a night school to which a limited number of the most promising of these men and women would be admitted on condition that they work ten hours during the day and attend school for two hours at night. They were to be paid something above the cost of their board. The greater part of their earnings was to be reserved in the school's treasury as a fund to be drawn on when they became day-school students. General Armstrong decided that the person to be put in charge of such a school was Booker Washington.

In the fall the Indians who had been under Washington's care were absorbed into the student body. The Negro students accepted the Indians as roommates and the Indians took their places in classrooms and shops. The first stage of Hampton's experiment had ended successfully. Hampton Institute was to educate many Indians after this group, but certainly much of the credit for later achievements must go to the Indians' first "house father."

While the student-teacher at Hampton guided the newly organized night classes, certain events took place in Macon County, Alabama, which determined the finished mold of Booker T. Washington's life. Macon County was part of the Black Belt famous for its large number of slaves and for the cotton they produced. The county seat was Tuskegee, most prosperous interior town of Alabama. From it had gone forth judges, Congressmen, and others representing the flower of Southern culture. Tuskegee was the residence of wealthy planters whose plantations extended over the surrounding country. On every plantation, in addition to "field hands" who worked in the cotton fields, were scores of black craftsmen who worked with lumber, stone, leather, tin, and mortar to meet the needs of plantation production. Inside the great colonial mansions a host of well-dressed dark-skinned maids, butlers, cooks, laundresses, coachmen, and stable boys were at the beck and call of the masters. Up to the very start of the war nothing in Macon County seemed more perpetual than black slavery.

War and the subsequent abolition of the institution of slavery changed everything. In the decade after the war Macon County sank farther and farther into the slough of sullen despondency and poverty. When by 1878 other sections of the country were showing unmistakable signs of recovery, feeble initiative began to stir in Macon County. Grave concern for the situation had come to take the place of disappointment and passion. Even the most vehement among the whites saw that something had to be done.

One former colonel in the Confederate army made a decisive break with the past. He decided to run for the state legislature and enlist the vote of the newly enfranchised freedman to win the seat from its long-intrenched and impotent occupant. Up to this time the ex-slaves in Macon County had not dared to use their vote. A certain Negro named Lewis Adams was well known to the Colonel as being unusually industrious, capable, and intelligent. He was a mechanic who had learned the trades of shoemaking, harnessmaking, and tinsmithing during the days of slavery. Most families in the region at some time or other called in Lewis Adams. If anyone could influence his own people, surely this man could. The former slaveholder had a talk with the former slave and asked him what he could do to secure the Negro vote promptly. Lewis Adams replied that what his race most wanted was education. If the Colonel would agree to work for the passage of a bill appropriating money for the maintenance of a school for Negroes, he, Adams, would help to get for him the Negro vote and the election.

The Colonel won the election and, being a true gentleman, proceeded to carry out his part of the bargain, with the happy result that early in the year 1881 two thousand dollars a year was appropriated by the legislature of Alabama for the establishment of a normal and industrial school for Negroes in the town of Tuskegee. The measure was passed, but with slight hope for its success. The two thousand dollars was set aside for teachers' salaries only. No land was provided; no buildings were bought or erected, no provisions made for the equipment of a school. Now, if the Negroes of Macon County wished to provide teachers and leaders for themselves, let them do so!

Lewis Adams was jubilant. An undulating wave of hope and joy passed over the poor hovels and shacks of Negroes in the region. Some white citizens were sympathetic, but to most of them the whole idea seemed rather silly. One, a merchant and banker of Tuskegee, George W. Campbell, believed that the plan should be given a chance. When Lewis Adams solicited his help, Mr. Campbell gladly agree to join with the ex-slave in exploring all possibilities.

In April, General Armstrong, at Hampton, received a letter from Alabama asking him to recommend someone to take charge of a projected normal school for Negroes in that state. Two thousand dollars had been appropriated for salary. The writers seemed to take it for granted that no Negro suitable for the position could be secured. They had been informed of the high quality of Hampton's teachers and hoped that the General might be able to recommend one of those who had been working with him in the great task of lifting the freedman.

After reading the letter the principal of Hampton sat for some time looking through his open window. This was great news—news which indicated that the influence of Hampton Institute was spreading over the land. Even the deepest South was awakening to its responsibility—was becoming aware that its own salvation lay in training its Negroes to become useful, hopeful citizens. General Armstrong read the letter through again; he drummed his fingers on the desk; then he sent for Booker Washington.

"Sit down," he said when the young man appeared. The instructor had evidently been interrupted in the midst of work. He was breathing heavily and he showed signs of nervousness. General Armstrong observed him closely for a moment, then said, "You've been working very hard, Mr. Washington. You're getting excellent results."

"I'm glad you think so, sir."

"How are you getting along in your advanced studies?"

"I think my teachers are—satisfied," was the modest reply.

General Armstrong smiled. "I'm quite sure you're correct in that assumption." He leaned forward. "Now let's see—you first entered Hampton in—"

"The fall of '72," Washington said.

"How old were you then?"

"Fifteen, sir."

General Armstrong frowned thoughtfully. "That makes you twenty-four years old now." He shook his head slowly. "You're still so young, my boy! You're too young for such a task."

Washington's face was anxious; his gray eyes looked puzzled. "What task, sir? I—I—love my work here."

"Read this letter." The principal handed the letter to him.

"This is wonderful, sir!" exclaimed Washington, lifting his eyes.

"I was thinking of recommending you," said General Armstrong quietly.

"Me! Me, sir!" The young man gaped at him in amazement.

"Would you go?"

"Why—why—if you thought— Of course," stammered Washington, "if you think I could fill such a position—it would —be—I don't know how to say it, sir," he finished lamely.

General Armstrong smiled. "I think you could do it. In fact, I know of no one anywhere whom I should consider better qualified to fill this position."

Washington walked from the principal's office in a daze. *To head a normal and industrial school—to head a school like*

Hampton—with a salary of two thousand dollars! The prospect made his head swim.

A week went by, and then on the first Sunday in May, shortly before sundown, students and faculty assembled in the chapel for vespers. This was a short service, but visitors always drove in from miles around just to hear the singing under Mr. Fenner's direction.

Vespers were nearly over when a messenger made his way to the platform as unobtrusively as possible and handed General Armstrong a yellow envelope. He tore open the telegram, read its contents, then covered his face with one hand and sat as if in prayer until the last song was completed. Immediately the General rose and came forward to the edge of the platform.

"I have an announcement to make which will interest students and faculty alike." The assembly swayed toward him as he told them of the letter from Alabama.

"The establishment of such a school in the deep South will be the most important step forward for a whole race since Emancipation Day. Hampton Institute is honored by this request coming from the state of Alabama." He paused and then continued solemnly. "I asked the guidance of my Heavenly Father in making this important recommendation and He led me to chose a member of your own race—one eminently prepared for such a task. He did not flinch or turn away when I called him, though you and I both know that one who goes into the deep South on such a mission takes his life in his hands. Our prayers will go with him. Hampton's loss will be the gain of those struggling in darkness." He paused as heads craned and a murmur rose. Many looked toward the young man halfway back in the chapel, his eyes lowered. General Armstrong's voice turned all eyes forward as he said, "I should now like to read you the telegram which I have just been handed. It reads:

'BOOKER T. WASHINGTON WILL SUIT US. SEND HIM AT ONCE.' "

In the hush which followed, Mr. Fenner rose quickly and signaled to the chorus. Suddenly the evening was filled with glorious organlike music that floated out through open win-

129

dows, across waters stained with the last rays of a setting sun, and up into a listening sky:

> "Go down, Moses,
> 'Way down in Egypt land,
> An' tell ole Pharaoh
> To let my people go!"

A deep, melodious baritone poured out the story, while the chorus chanted the injunction:

> "Thus spoke the Lord, bold Moses said,
> Let my people go!
> If not, I'll smite your first-born dead.
> Let my people go!"

With a spontaneous impulse the entire assembly rose to its feet. Every Hampton student threw back his head, then opened his heart and gave it in liquid form to this one of their own who was going forth to lead his people out of the mire and degredation in which two hundred years of slavery had buried them:

> "Go down, Moses,
> 'Way down in Egypt land,
> An' tell ole Pharaoh
> To let my people go!"

Part III

BEHOLD THE LAND!

❖◇❖

You are my South—
I'll hammer you
Into a beautiful song
For I love you.
        —Don West

11

July 4, 1881

"Gawd bless you', Mistah Washin'ton! Jus' yo' tell me what kin Ah do fur da school."

She must have been a hundred years old as she stood there peering up at him with keen black eyes. Her face was criss-crossed with wrinkles, she was bent and twisted like an ancient tree, but the old lady gripped her knotted stick firmly and her voice was eager as a young girl's.

Washington smiled and patted the frail shoulder. "Thank you, Grannie," he said. "Thank you kindly. I'll be stopping by to see you real soon."

He trudged on down the dusty road with the old lady's blessings sounding in his ears. Ahead of him a tall poplar reached for the sky. From the shrub entwined about its trunk hung sprays of tiny white flowers that filled the air with per-fume. Flowering vines climbed over fallen fences and trans-formed hovels which were hardly more than rotting sticks leaning together—hovels and shacks swarming with skinny, pot-bellied, dusky children who gazed at him with round, im-ploring eyes.

Despair was in his heart that June day. He had traveled southward with wings on his heels and rainbows wrapped about his shoulders. He was going to be a fine, conscientious participant in Alabama's newest and most worthy educational endeavor. He found nothing—no school building—no slightest space—nothing except this host of poverty-stricken, anxious black folk who had been told that he would give them a school for teachers and leaders.

As he walked through the streets of Tuskegee or traveled

over the country roads, sometimes astride a mule, sometimes in a cart beside a proud and talkative driver, sometimes on foot, Washington knew that he was regarded with suspicion and even abhorrence by most of the white people. He was that most reprehensible of creatures, an "educated n———" They feared that bringing such a person into the community could result only in serious trouble between themselves and the blacks. Not even the banker and merchant, Mr. George W. Campbell, had yet been able to mobilize support for the project among Tuskegee's old residents. Mr. Campbell warned Washington to "go slow; don't irritate the families whose support you must have."

Washington's face was grim as his eyes swept over a big colonial house sitting well behind a row of fine old sycamore trees.

"I'll be visiting you yet, Colonel," he promised in a whisper. "I'll prove to you that educating Negroes is a good thing for everything *you value so much."*

A few minutes later the young man turned off down a side road. He was on his way to visit a group of Negro tenant farmers whose poor plots were well hidden from the Big House by a grove of pine trees.

The Alabama Constitution of 1876 established the first public schools for white and Negro children. Macon County planters swore they would have nothing to do with such carpetbagger measures. Alabama's first Superintendent of Public Instruction reported, "When I began operations in Macon County, I found great hostility to our free public school system. It was a hard matter to find trustees in every township who would take sufficient interest to establish colored schools."

In time a few abandoned cabins were declared schoolhouses. The first teachers were courageous Negroes from Northern high schools who, with few books and no equipment, endeavored to set up standard curriculums. Results would have been slow and difficult at best, but these teachers were driven out along with all other reconstruction directors. Where the schools for Negro children were not wiped out altogether, they

134

were turned over to teachers whose contacts with education had been vague and uncertain.

When Booker T. Washington arrived in Alabama he faced a situation which might well have seemed hopeless. Yet, though he floundered about, it did not occur to him to run away. The need for his kind of school bound him to the task. This need cried out to him on every hand. He had to find a place where he could work. He had to find strong, alert young Negro men and women whom he could train quickly and send back to disseminate what they had learned; to teach people how to grow food, how to build houses, how to rescue the children of the race from extinction.

And so he took his case directly to the people whom he hoped to serve. He ate and slept with them in their cabins, asked questions, and talked to them of their children's future. They welcomed him gladly and contrived some place in their one room for him, either on the floor or in a special part of another's bed. They listened eagerly to what he had to say, then sent him farther up the road—always with some useful knowledge, some valuable word of advice, a promise to "help da school."

He found them living almost solely on a diet of fat pork and corn bread. The meal from which the bread was baked was being bought at a high price at a store in town, although the land all about could easily have been made to produce every kind of vegetable. Instead, cotton was planted to the very door of their cabins.

Many of the Negroes had been warned against him. In addition to whites who told them "We don't need no meddling outsiders round here," their preachers distrusted the stranger with probing gray eyes who asked so many questions. He did not come "bringin' da Gospel," they said. He did not speak of "hebben" or "sin." The story was circulated how when a white minister in town addressed the newcomer as "Reverend" he quickly disclaimed all right to that honorable title. The white minister was taken somewhat aback. He thought all spokesmen for Negroes called themselves preachers.

Yet it was in a tumble-down Methodist church and its adjacent woodshed that Booker T. Washington's first "Tuskegee Institute" was housed. Lewis Adams had his own circuitous methods of securing what he went after, and his arguments finally prevailed upon the elders.

"We got a place, Mr. Washington!" Adams was triumphant. When the young man's face beamed with joy, he added hastily, " 'Course it ain't so much, but we can open our school."

Church and shed were sadly in need of repairs. But Washington consoled himself with the thought that he and his students would soon put everything in order. He announced that the "Normal and Industrial School" would open July 4th, Independence Day. Then, with the help of Adams' two boys, he set about cleaning up the place.

"Pa, he's a funny kind o' teachah," Frank Adams told his father.

Lewis Adams scratched his head reflectively. The shrewd, tireless workman had never been to school a day in his life. During slavery he had somehow managed to teach himself to read and write. Frankly he had expected something more impressive for their money than the smooth-faced, rather bashful young man Hampton Institute had sent.

Now he nodded his head slowly and agreed, "Yes, son, he sho is—no high collar, no fancy boots, no big words. He's awful slow at talkin'. But, boy, Ah sho laks the way he goes about *doin'* things. Ah think he's gonna set us up a fine school!" And Lewis Adams went out to round up Tuskegee's leading citizens for the "grand opening."

It rained in the Tuskegee valley on July 4, 1881. Water came down in bucketfuls. Farmers rejoiced. Such a rain was unusual before the long summer drought. The head of the "Normal and Industrial School for Colored" delivered his opening address standing under an umbrella which the faithful Lewis Adams held open to protect him from the downpour coming through the roof over his head. Thirty students had reported for admission. With them had come about an equal number of well-wishers and the curious. They huddled together under open umbrellas or crouched in corners which offered some refuge from the steadily leaking roof. As Washington conscientiously set forth the purposes of the new school, the rain formed in little puddles about their feet. When the speaker concluded, they stood up and in weak, faraway voices sang: "My Country, 'Tis of Thee, Sweet Land of Liberty, Of Thee I sing."

Far away, "up no'th," Miss Olivia A. Davidson, recent graduate of Massachusetts State Normal School at Framingham, Massachusetts, stood up respectfully when Mrs. Mary Hemenway entered the drawing room.

"My dear Miss Davidson," exclaimed the Boston matron cordially, "I am so glad you called! How are you and what are you doing in Boston? Sit down, my dear, and tell me about yourself."

"I couldn't miss this opportunity, Mrs. Hemenway, to come and thank you once more for all you've done for me." The young woman's voice was pleasantly modulated. Her large brown eyes gave beauty to an otherwise plain, angular face. A slight flush added color to a sallow skin only one shade darker than Mrs. Hemenway's.

"Your fine record at Framingham has repaid me a hundredfold, Miss Davidson," Mrs. Hemenway told her graciously. "We're all very proud of you. And now what? Do you have a teaching position?"

"I've applied for a job in Cincinnati. That's very close to my home. My mother is getting along in years and I'd like to be near her."

"Your mother isn't ill?" asked Mrs. Hemenway quickly.

"Oh, no, ma'am. We have our little house in Westwood, where she's quite comfortable. Her garden and a few chickens keep her just busy enough."

"I'm glad to hear you say that because—well—as a matter of fact, I received a letter from General Armstrong this week which mentioned you. I was going to write you." She leaned forward. "And now you're here!"

"General Armstrong had a position in mind for me?"

"It seems that one of our most promising Hampton graduates has just opened a Normal and Industrial School for colored people in Alabama. The General writes most hopefully of the undertaking and says he would like me to send him a helper—someone thoroughly qualified to train teachers along the lines Hampton is following." The lady smiled brightly. "He suggested you."

Olivia Davidson looked down at her folded hands. She had been born in Ohio and received her elementary education in the public schools of that state. Upon graduation from high school and while still in her teens she had gone to Mississippi to teach in the newly organized schools for Negroes. When colored schools no longer had the protection of troops stationed there, she went to Memphis, Tennessee, where she continued teaching until all schools were closed by an epidemic of yellow fever. She offered her services as a nurse. By this time she knew that she needed to be better qualified to prepare her pupils for life in their communities. She heard of Hampton Institute and arrived there in the fall of 1878 and was at once admitted to the graduating class. Her unusual work that year attracted attention. Upon her graduation in 1879 one of Hampton's most ardent sponsors recommended that this graduate enter the Normal School in Massachusetts. Mrs. Mary Hemenway backed her recommendation by assuming the financial obligation for Olivia Davidson's two-year course at Framingham.

Now, after only a moment's reflection, Olivia Davidson lifted her brown eyes and asked, "Where did General Armstrong say the school is?"

"It's an Indian name—let's see—Tuskaloo, or Oskegee, something like that. I'll get the letter."

"Oh, please, ma'am, don't disturb yourself. I'll write General Armstrong for details. Of course I *am* interested. I wonder if I know the one who is heading the school."

"Perhaps not. He's been at Hampton these past two years taking advanced studies and teaching. Everybody speaks most highly of him. His name is Washington. I remember his name because it's rather odd—Booker Washington."

Tuskegee Normal and Industrial School took on new life

with the arrival of Miss Davidson the first week in September. Where Washington had been carefully feeling his way, moving cautiously and deliberately, Miss Davidson sailed in with a cheerful assurance which was disarming. The old church no longer leaked and sagged, but very soon it seemed in danger of bursting at the seams. The school lacked everything except students, who continued to multiply until the new lady principal pleasantly but firmly announced that all classes were full. Books, blackboards, other school equipment was needed. With the help of women students Miss Davidson planned a number of "suppers." She called on white and colored families in the town and asked them to give something—a cake, a chicken, bread, or pies—which could be sold at the supper. The first of these affairs was a great success. It was in the evening. People came out of curiosity and stayed to chat with students and to buy some of the good things spread out on tables in the church-yard.

"Now we can buy blackboards," Washington said that night when they counted the proceeds from the food sales. The heavy sigh with which he followed his declaration brought Miss Davidson's eyes to his face.

"You don't sound very cheerful about it," she gently chided.

"I'm sorry, Miss Davidson. I know how hard you worked. But"—he slapped his hand against the table—"what can we do cooped up here? We need space to set our students to *doing*. They're anxious enough to learn, but most of our pupils come from the country. We want them to know the importance of farm life."

"We do need much more than blackboards and books. I know that, Mr. Washington, and yet—" She stopped and smiled.

Washington stood up and she thought, *How very young he is!* He saw her smile and was ashamed of his impatience. "We do need blackboards and books, Miss Davidson. We're making progress."

About a week later Mr. Washington heard that an abandoned plantation of five hundred acres lying just outside Tuskegee was coming up for sale. Jeff Thompkins, Negro proprie-

139

tor of the only hardware store in the town, brought him the information.

"Five hundred dollars is all they's askin' for hit, Mr. Washington, an'—even bad as things is round here—that's mighty cheap."

Washington laughed. "I don't have five hundred dollars, Mr. Thompkins, but I sure would like to have five hundred acres for our school."

When he mentioned the sale to Miss Davidson she said, "Let's go and see it!"

Jeff Thompkins drove them out in his wagon. Only the charred ruins of the Big House remained. The original separate kitchen, a stable and a henhouse, a cluster of rickety slave cabins remained. The fields had been used and reused until the soil had lost most of its fertility, yet it was good. Fertilization could make it productive. There was plenty of woodland well covered with trees; there were meadows and pastureland, and there was water.

The two teachers returned to town, their eyes swimming with visions. Washington went immediately to the banker, Mr. Campbell, and asked him to speak with the owner in behalf of the school.

"You understand, Washington," Mr. Campbell explained, "no part of the state's appropriation can be used for such a purchase."

"I understand, sir," Washington answered. "We thought that if the owner were willing to trust us for a period we might be able to raise the money."

"Raise five hundred dollars?" Mr. Campbell looked skeptical.

The land-poor owner was open to reason. He agreed to let the teachers take their school out to his place if they made a down payment of two hundred and fifty dollars and agreed to pay the remaining two hundred and fifty dollars within a year.

"Mighty good terms, Washington," declared Mr. Campbell. "I'd say those were mighty good terms!"

It was Miss Davidson who suggested that Hampton Institute might lend him the two hundred and fifty dollars. Washington stared at her in amazement, but he mustered his courage and addressed a letter to Mr. Marshall, treasurer of Hampton Institute, explaining the circumstances and asking if such a loan might be possible. A reply came back within a few days. Mr. Marshall said he had no authority to lend money belonging to Hampton Institute, but he would gladly lend Mr. Washington the amount needed from his own funds.

"I can't believe it!" gasped Washington.

"Why not?" asked Miss Davidson. "Well, Mr. Washington, when do we move?"

"Cotton picking time" in the Black Belt began in September and continued almost until "da Christmas." No colored schools were open during this period since Negro children were needed in the cotton fields. The bulk of the students at the new Normal and Industrial School were public schoolteachers, some of them forty years old. Washington now faced the problem of mobilizing his entire student body to get the new location ready for school purposes. He went about it in the only way he knew: first, he explained the need; second, he took up an ax, a shovel, and a hoe and went to work himself. Not all students followed suit at once. Some of them grumbled that they had come to "college" not to clean henhouses and repair pigsties. But excitement grew around the town. People drove out to the "old Hube place" to see what was going on; offers of help were made and gratefully accepted. Before long the cabins were in usable condition; stable and henhouse were set up as recitation rooms; the old kitchen was restored. One room had been salvaged from the gutted mansion. This would be the Assembly Hall.

One afternoon when Miss Davidson was busy setting up blackboards she heard, "Miss Davidson, look quick! Yondoh come Mistah Washin'ton with a hoss!"

She hurried to the door and stood staring as the principal came up the path leading a horse which stumbled and swayed with age. Washington's usually sober face was beaming.

"Here we are, Miss Davidson," he called out when he saw her. "The school's first animal! One of the white citizens of Tuskegee gave me this!" He halted and surveyed his gift with happy affection.

Miss Davidson stepped outside. She walked around the

141

horse, slowly inspecting it. She paused suddenly, waved her hand before the animal's eyes, and exclaimed, "Why, Mr. Washington, this poor creature's blind!"

Washington frowned. His voice was nettled. "What if it is? It's got four legs, hasn't it?" And without another word he led his horse away.

Miss Davidson looked after him soberly. She wondered where the principal would house his livestock. She and her students were using the stable.

The next weeks flew by. Washington went out to live on the plantation as soon as he could fix up one of the cabins. He was up at dawn and did not go to bed until he was exhausted. Within a short time several of the cabins were brought together, side walls knocked out, and living quarters of a sort made for twenty or twenty-five people. Miss Davidson and the more courageous students moved in. The old kitchen was restored, pots and pans were assembled, and once more the chimney began to smoke. After classes Washington led the young men to the woods and fields, where they worked until sundown. Then they returned to eat a meal prepared and served by Miss Davidson and the women students.

This was indeed a new kind of school. People in Tuskegee and the surrounding country who had been hostile to the idea of having a Negro school in their midst were pleasantly surprised. The old plantation which for so long had been a desolate wilderness took on a new aspect which suggested progress. Fresh movements stirred throughout the region.

Washington was hardly aware of the passage of time until one day he received a letter from his sister, Mandy, telling him she was coming down for a visit during the Christmas vacation.

"Everybody here is so excited about your school that John says he'll send me for a week's visit," wrote Mandy. "I'ı bringing another student with me. She's been working anc saving her money for the trip. We know you'll be needing more teachers very soon, so we'll get our application in early."

"What shall we do with two more girls?" asked Washington.

"That's easy," replied Miss Davidson cheerfully. "The two

women in my cabin are going home for Christmas. I'll take the visitors in with me."

Christmas had meant very little to the miners in West Virginia. But Christmas throughout the Black Belt was looked forward to all year long. Even in slavery times all work stopped the day before Christmas. Restrictions were relaxed. Christmas was a time for hilarity.

Lewis Adams drove Washington to Chehaw on Christmas Eve to meet the train bringing Mandy and her friend.

"Mah wife's right pleased yo' all havin' Christmas dinnah with us, Mr. Washington. Hit's mighty nice of yo' sistah to come all dis way to be with yo'." Lewis Adams' face was wreathed in smiles. He was very proud of the Hampton graduate now. Any visitors from Hampton would be welcomed in Tuskegee.

The train was late, as always, and Washington paced impatiently up and down the track. Chehaw was little more than a collection of empty warehouses and storage bins. It was a whistle stop for the trains. At one time a branch line had run to Tuskegee, but this track had long since been demolished.

At last they heard the train coming out of the dusk, and the long beam of the headlight lit the buggy and made the horse shy away. The wheels ground to a stop; a brakeman with lantern swung to the ground. Washington hurried toward the car from which three passengers alighted: one man, and Mandy—and there, her face uplifted, her eyes dancing, her dimples showing as the brakeman held his lantern high, was Fannie Smith!

"Howdee, Mr. Teacher," she said in her warm, throaty voice.

His heart turned over with sheer joy. He knew suddenly that this would be the most wonderful Christmas in the world!

12

Bricks Without Straw

Washington knew that the new year would be a good one. He knew it by the buoyancy of his whole body. He knew it by the way the soil turned on his spade, by the feel of the wind on his face. He knew it by the ready response given to their plea for money to purchase the land.

"This is your school! What will you give to help?"

For the most part, the money came in small dribbles—a dollar here, a dollar there. Many did not have money, but they gave what they had.

"Ah'm savin' one egg eve'y day fur yo', Mistah Washin'ton. Jus' yo drop by fur it. Dat egg's fur da school!"

Some brought a few potatoes, some a long stalk of sugar cane, some a small bag of grits.

Dr. Washington told about these beginnings in his *Up from Slavery:*

> From the first I resolved to make the school a real part of the community in which it was located. I was determined that no one should have the feeling that it was a foreign institution, dropped down in the midst of the people, for which they had no responsibility and in which they had no interest. I noticed that the very fact that they had been asked to contribute toward the purchase of the land made them begin to feel as if it was going to be their school. I noted that just in proportion as we made the white people feel that the institution was a part of the life of the community, and that we wanted to make the school of real service to all the people, their attitude toward the school became favourable.

144

One morning about the middle of January the school had a visitor. He appeared unannounced and sat down in the back of the stable-recitation room where Miss Davidson was conducting a class.

"Don't let me disturb you, Teacher," he said in a pleasant drawl when Miss Davidson approached him. "Mind if I listen?"

"Oh, no indeed, sir. This is a geography class." Miss Davidson smiled. "We're studying the state of Alabama."

"I'm Georgia-born, Teacher," the visitor told her. "I reckon I better listen to this."

Miss Davidson went on with her work. As quietly as he had appeared the visitor slipped out.

Washington saw the white man standing at the corner of a field which half a dozen students were clearing of several years' growth of scrub brush, thistles, and weeds. The man was so absorbed in what he was seeing that he did not notice Washington coming toward him.

He turned quickly when he heard the cordial "Good morning, sir. I'm Booker Washington. Can I be of service to you?"

The visitor's blue eyes crinkled. "I should have known you from my friend Mr. Campbell's description. You *are* very young."

Washington's smile was a trifle crooked. He never thought of himself as being "very young."

He passed over the observation without comment and said, instead, "Mr. Campbell has surely been my friend, sir, and the friend of our school. May I show you around?"

"I'm Jabez Curry, live in Talladega County. Been hearing about what you all were doing down here. Thought I'd drop in and see for myself. Must say it looks fine."

"We're only making a beginning, sir." Washington waved his hand toward the field. "We hope to plow this all up and get it under cultivation soon, so as to secure some return from it and at the same time give the students training in agriculture."

"Very good. Very good indeed! I understand you made the down payment on the land from your own pocket, Washington." Mr. Curry spoke casually.

"I was very fortunate in being able to borrow the amount,"

Washington told him modestly. He smiled. "I didn't have that much in my own pocket."

"But it's your personal loan. You'll have to pay it back yourself until the money is raised," insisted the other.

"Oh, but we'll get it, sir!" Washington said enthusiastically, and told how the money was slowly but steadily coming in.

The visitor watched the young man's face while he talked.

"And then what?" he asked.

Washington's voice was apologetic. "Of course, Mr. Curry, we need everything—plows and mules and carts. But all I can think of at the moment is that we must start erecting a building as soon as possible."

They walked together up the slope to where the Big House had once stood. All the charred timbers had been removed. Two young men were busy whitewashing the restored walls of what was now their Assembly Hall.

After a few more questions Mr. Curry drove away. If Washington was disappointed because the visitor made no contribution to the work, he consoled himself by thinking, *I'm sure we've made another friend.*

Ten days later as he was hurrying through the center of town Washington heard someone calling to him. He turned and saw Mr. Campbell, who had pulled his buggy to a stop and was waving his whip.

"Just a minute, young man! I've good news for you." The merchant-banker sounded jubilant.

Washington hurried to the side of the buggy.

"How do you do, Mr. Campbell. I didn't see you."

"That's all right, Washington. You're a busy man. Well, let me tell you that your two-thousand-dollar annual appropriation has been increased to three thousand—beginning *this month!*"

"Oh! Oh, sir!" Washington couldn't say anything else.

"Yes! You see, J. L. M. Curry is general agent of the Peabody Fund. That fund has recently been set up for the express purpose of aiding educational institutions. This additional one thousand dollars is the result of Mr. Curry's report to the Peabody Assembly. You and your school made quite an impression on the Peabody agent!"

Yes, it was a good year. Three months after Mr. Marshall made his generous loan, Washington paid it back. Seven months after the owner of the land agreed to let the school take over the plantation, he received his final payment of two hundred and fifty dollars.

After the classes closed in June, the head of Tuskegee Normal and Industrial School declared a week's vacation for himself. He traveled back to Malden and there, in a little cottage on the edge of town, Reverend Johnson married Miss Fannie N. Smith and Booker T. Washington. Everybody wanted them to have a church wedding. The young man patiently explained that there was no time. Fannie did not care. Her happiness bubbled over in her voice, her eyes, her walk. Her father, one of the small farmers who had settled in the Kanawha valley before the war, was proud of his daughter. Her mother, a wren-like little brown woman, cried when the young husband took her daughter away, but her heart was filled with thanksgiving. Fannie was so lovely, so pretty, so capricious that her mother had worried about her. Now all was well.

Back in Tuskegee, Washington led his bride into a freshly modeled cabin. Its two rooms were bright with paint and varnish. Its fittings were crude but adequate. There was no kitchen. All cooking had to be done in the big school kitchen.

Now the young man was wholly content. Surely no man on earth had so much as he! Not only were all things possible but they were being accomplished. He threw himself into plans for the new building as confidently as he dropped seeds into the ground. According to Dr. Emmett J. Scott, who for many years was Washington's closest associate, in these days Washington first began "putting his hand on anything he wanted round the town." Later he put his hand on anything he wanted throughout the county, then the state. Finally he put his hand on anything he wanted throughout the country.

The story is told of how, at a meeting called to discuss ways and means of raising funds for the school, an old ex-slave came twelve miles to bring a large hog in his ox cart. In the midst of the discussion he rose and said he had no money to give but that he had raised two fine hogs, and that he had brought one of them as a contribution toward the expenses of the new building. He closed this announcement with: "Anybody that's got love for his race, or respect for himself, will bring a hog to the next meeting."

As soon as plans for the new building were completed, students began breaking the ground for the foundations. They worked after classes were over. Then came the day set for laying the cornerstone.

People came from far and near, for by this time interest in the school was statewide. It was a beautiful fall day—just one year after Washington had taken up his abode in the cabin behind the charred ruins of the plantation mansion—when teachers, students and their parents, white county officials and other leading white men of the vicinity gathered with black men and women whom they had once held in bondage. Only sixteen years before, it was illegal to teach a Negro to read or write in Macon County. Now they watched the cornerstone laid for an institution to train teachers; they heard an address delivered by Mr. Waddy Thompson, Superintendent of Education; all bowed their heads while a Negro preacher thanked God for this "great day."

Fannie flitted about in the crowd seeing that all went well. Refreshments were served from long tables set up under the trees. She saw to it that visitors were steered in that direction. Every time Washington caught a glimpse of his wife, happiness flooded his being.

"Well, Washington"—the young husband took his eyes off Fannie and turned to smile at Mr. Campbell—"we're proud of you! This turnout is a real tribute to you."

"Thank you, sir. I don't know how to tell you how grateful I am."

The Superintendent of Schools joined them and exclaimed, "I see the plans for your building call for brick."

"Yes, indeed, sir," said Washington. "We plan a fine brick building."

Mr. Thompson shook his head. "I fear you've been badly

148

advised in this, Washington. That's going to be mighty expensive."

Mr. Campbell cut in. "I think you'll see that our principal has figured that all out."

"But there's not a brickyard in this part of the state," declared Mr. Thompson. "The shipping cost will make your bricks cost double."

Washington smiled. "Not our bricks, sir."

"Where on earth are you going to get them?"

"We're going to make them, sir!"

This was Washington's plan for solving the shortage in bricks. He had discovered excellent brick clay on the place and decided that, in addition to filling their own needs, they could sell bricks for the general market.

The undertaking was harder than he had anticipated. He soon learned that special skill and knowledge were required, particularly for baking the bricks. He finally found a man who said he had this special knowledge; but when it came to brickmaking, the students' distaste for manual labor along with book education became clearly manifest. It was not a pleasant task to stand in the mud pit for hours, with mud up to the knees. Many men became disgusted and left the school.

At last, after weeks of back-breaking effort, twenty-five thousand bricks were molded and put into the kiln to be baked.

They were reduced to a powdery white dust! The kiln had not been properly constructed. Washington and the students mended the kiln and tried again, with the same result.

The entire school was reduced to hopeless despair—all except the principal.

"We have failed," he said, "because of our ignorance. And so we have learned a lesson. I have sent a telegram to Hampton Institute, where brickmaking is taught by experts. Hampton turns out good bricks. We shall learn how to make a kiln before we try any more bricks."

Hampton could spare three men who volunteered their services. Weeks had been consumed in fruitless effort, and the Christmas holiday was so close that it was decided the Hampton men should not come until the second week in January.

The heavy gloom over Tuskegee lifted. For the first time in weeks, students talked about something other than bricks. People in town knew about the failure of the kiln. They were divided in their opinion as to the wisdom of sending "up North" for help, but nobody blamed Booker Washington.

"Nothin' bows his head," boasted Lewis Adams. "He'll make his bricks yet!"

People did not know the deep joy which lay behind the calm gray eyes, for Fannie was going to have a baby. As she grew more beautiful in his eyes, Washington thought of his mother, understood her great love, and hoped that she knew of his happiness.

"Our child—born in freedom!" He whispered the words and held Fannie close.

The days flew by on wings. The Hampton experts arrived and once more a batch of bricks was made and put in the kiln. They had to bake for six days. Never were fires watched more anxiously. "How the bricks coming?" was the most frequent question asked on all sides. Three, four, five days went by. The tension eased. At last they would have bricks for the new building. Nothing further could be done on it until the bricks were ready.

Washington went to bed earlier than usual that night. He and Fannie lay in the darkness talking of the new building, of the baby, of the baby's future. He fell into a deep, dreamless slumber.

Somebody was knocking on the door! Pounding! Calling!

"Mr. Washington! Come quick! The kiln!"

He sprang up—groping for his clothes—his first reaction anger that Fannie had been wakened.

She rose quickly, lit the lamp with deft fingers, and called, "All right. Mr. Washington is coming."

"What is it?" he asked the panting boy.

"Look like the whole kiln fell in."

For the third time they had failed. Now the experts were confounded. They could say nothing until the kiln had cooled and they could get inside and examine it. Only one thing was certain—the bricks would be no good.

Miss Davidson shook her head at breakfast. Her eyes were red. "It's no good, Mr. Washington," she said. "We'll have to give up trying to make bricks."

Washington's mouth was set in a hard, grim line. He gulped down a cup of coffee and hurried back to the kiln.

Later that morning he told Fannie, "I'm going to Montgomery. Every dollar's gone and we must have money right away. I think I know someone in the city who will help us in this emergency." He kissed her quickly and was gone.

The month after Christmas is a poor time for raising money. Washington had the names of several men in Montgomery who had declared themselves friends of the school, but none of them had money for the materials which the Hampton brickmakers had said were necessary for reenforcing the kiln.

"It's a crazy idea, Teacher," said one merchant impatiently. "You can't make bricks out of that mud. You all made a fine start. Now just stick to your farming and leave brickmaking alone."

Washington walked down the street pondering this advice. He thought of all the straggling farms he had seen between Tuskegee and Montgomery; he thought of all the broken fences, tumble-down shacks, and—

He stopped, his eyes on the window of a pawnshop. He had one thing he might pawn! He turned and quickly entered the shop.

The shopkeeper looked over the customer before speaking. He was not the type of Negro who frequented his shop. He might have something worth while.

"What do you want, boy?" he asked.

This form of address was customary when a white man in the deep South spoke to a Negro, whatever his age might be. Washington did not reply. He laid his gold watch on the counter.

It was his only valuable possession. He had bought it at the end of his last good season at Narragansett Pier. The watch had been his one touch of elegance that winter in Washington. It had given him confidence when he went back to teach at Hampton Institute. It seemed indispensable now for keeping strict schedule at Tuskegee. The gold watch was undoubtedly an emblem. He laid it on the counter and waited.

The shopkeeper picked it up. His eyes veiled as he turned the watch in his hands. It was a good watch—a very good watch.

"You want to pawn this?" he asked while he considered.

"What will you let me have on it?" asked Washington.

"Fifteen dollars," came the reply.

"Fifteen dollars!" Considering what he had paid for it, Washington expected much more.

"Fifteen dollars," repeated the shopkeeper firmly.

Washington took the fifteen dollars along with a ticket which stated that he could redeem the watch within thirty days. He bought two items specified by his brickmakers and hurried back to Tuskegee. The experts rebuilt the kiln.

Somehow the discouraged forces were pulled together. For the fourth time the kiln was filled with bricks.

The bricks came out in perfect form! Everybody in the school assisted in piling them up in beautiful, neat rows. The very next day masons were fitting them into the wall of the new building.

Now it was time to plant. In the midst of putting in their first crops, supervising the erection of the building, and performing countless other duties, the thirty days allowed for his watch expired. These were days when dollars went out much faster than they came in. Miss Davidson decided to go North for the purpose of securing funds. For weeks she visited individuals, spoke in churches and before organizations. After a time they began to receive checks from her in the mail. It was the middle of March before Washington got back to Montgomery and the pawnshop.

"I've sold the watch," the pawnbroker told him curtly.

Washington consoled himself with the thought that now the kiln was turning out good bricks regularly.

He patted his empty pocket and murmured, "After the baby's born I'll get another watch."

He bought a little locket for Fannie and hurried home.

The new building was called Porter Hall, after Mr. A. H. Porter of Brooklyn, New York, who gave a generous sum toward its erection. Even before it was completed a portion was occupied by boarding students. They were now coming from such distances and in such increasing numbers that it was necessary to set up a regular boarding department. No provision had been made in the new building for a kitchen and a dining room. Again Principal Washington called on students to volunteer for work, this time to assist in digging out a basement. In a few weeks they had made a partially lighted basement room that could be used for cooking, with a section partitioned off for a dining room.

All the land was green and flowering when Fannie's baby was born on the first day of May. Fannie's eyes shone like stars in her haggard face and her blue lips smiled. The new father knelt beside her bed, his body shaken by the long-drawn-out suffering he had witnessed.

"You're all right now, Fannie, my darling; you're all right," he whispered.

She tried to nod her head. Her lips formed the words "Our baby!"

The old woman laid the newborn child beside her. Washington gazed at them in awe. He was afraid to touch his tiny daughter. Then the old woman said he must go away and let his wife rest.

No doctor in the Black Belt ever attended a Negro woman in childbirth. The old woman now attending Fannie did her best. But for months the baby had been draining the mother's life away. Without proper care the shock of the birth had been too much and Booker Washington's lovely little flower was fading.

She did not want to die. Life and love were so wonderful. Booker needed her—the baby needed her. She clung to them both as long as she could. She left them on May 10, 1884.

13

Tea With the Queen

"Teacher, wise helper of his race; good servant of God and country." With these words Charles W. Eliot, President of Harvard University, clasped the brown hand. The distinguished audience gathered in Sanders Theatre for Harvard University's two hundred and forty-ninth commencement surged forward, every eye focused on the platform.

"Booker Taliaferro Washington, Master of Arts!" pronounced President Eliot.

Then came the applause, not reluctant and stiff, but warm and enthusiastic. People spoke his name aloud and linked it with the word Tuskegee. The applause swept from pit to gallery while faces glowed with appreciation for the ex-slave whom Harvard now honored so singularly. Never before this morning of June 24, 1896, had Harvard University conferred an honorary degree upon a Negro.

He marched out into the morning sunshine, the black gown swirling about his feet, the hard mortarboard perched perilously on his head. By his side walked the elderly inventor Alexander Graham Bell, who had been honored by Harvard University for having given the telephone to the world.

Later at the Alumni Dinner in Memorial Hall, President Eliot introduced the speakers: Massachusetts Governor Roger Wolcott, Henry Cabot Lodge, and Booker T. Washington.

The hall was very still as Washington told them briefly:

"If through me, a humble representative, seven millions of my people in the South might be permitted to send a message to Harvard—Harvard that offered up on death's altar young Shaw, and Russell, and Lowell, and scores of others, that we

154

might have a free and united country—that message would be: 'Tell them that the sacrifice was not in vain. Tell them that by way of the shop, the field, the skilled hand, habits of thrift and economy; by way of industrial school and college, we are coming. We are crawling up, working up; yea, bursting up. Often through oppression, unjust discrimination, and prejudice; but through them all we are coming up, and with proper habits, intelligence, and property there is no power on earth that can permanently stay our progress!' "

Washington left Cambridge immediately after the dinner. He was speaking in Brooklyn the following night. Then he went to Philadelphia, out to Chicago and from there to St. Louis— always to appear before large audiences, always to seek out wealthy philanthropists in the interest of Tuskegee Institute.

A speech delivered eight months before at the mercantile Atlanta Exposition was the fortuitous circumstance which emblazoned Booker T. Washington's name across the nation. Through the New York *Tribune,* former Governor Bullock of Georgia announced that the purpose of the exposition was to prove to Northern capitalists that anti-Negro agitation was not truly representative of the South. "Our exposition," he wrote, "will dissipate the political usefulness of the color-line bugaboo and set our white people free to form and act upon their best judgment as to governmental policies, uncontrolled by prejudices engendered by issues that are now happily of the past." He assured New York businessmen that all was well in the South, and that "the colored labor of our section is the best, safest and most conservative in the world."

It was news when the Negro principal of an Alabama school was invited to speak at an exposition held in the deep South and managed by a board of "bank presidents, wholesale dealers, manufacturers and retired capitalists." It was sensational news when that Negro's speech amplified and dramatized Governor Bullock's announcement.

Washington's admonition to "Let down your buckets where you are!" and his declaration that "In all things that are purely social we can be as separate as the fingers, yet one as the hand in all things essential to mutual progress" were generally inter-

155

preted throughout the land as an injunction to Negroes to work and stop complaining and as an assurance to whites that Negroes did not need or desire "social equality."

Overnight Atlanta catapulted Booker T. Washington from obscurity to fame. He was hailed everywhere as the strong, wise leader of his race, not militant as the Abolitionist Frederick Douglass had been, not critical as the younger W. E. B. Du Bois.

Washington cared only that at last his work had attracted nationwide attention. The railroad quickly replaced its branch line from Chehaw to Tuskegee; money began pouring in to the school. This was all that mattered to Washington. Every hour of the day and night he was the "head of Tuskegee," a symbol, a spokesman, a slave to the work which he believed would lift his people from the depths. The school had been a hard taskmaster. Two years after Fannie's death he had married Miss Davidson. She planned and taught and directed, kept up her habit of going North to secure funds, unselfishly poured out her life during those arduous, anxious years while they made the school. She gave him two sons and died in 1889.

When the twice-bereaved husband stood beside the grave of Olivia Davidson Washington he had groaned, "It takes everything—everything from me!"

Now Alabama boasted of its Normal and Industrial Institute for Negroes, and all the South pointed with pride to Tuskegee. Dozens of brick buildings stood on the old plantation knoll; a thousand acres of land were being cultivated by students of agriculture. Each year from Tuskegee went forth teachers, carpenters, tinsmiths, dairymen, fruit growers, young women trained in nursing and every detail of homemaking. Always there was some new building going up. Always a new course was being planned. Always new students came in ever-increasing numbers. Tuskegee Institute never closed. Its principal never took a vacation.

As Washington's carriage approached the high grilled gates on a pleasant mid-July morning, the cadets stood straight as ramrods at the posts. The officer-of-the-day clicked his heels smartly and saluted. Washington returned the salute stiffly, then as the carriage rolled through the gate he looked back and smiled. The sight of his trim cadets always pleased him. He had been gone for three weeks, traveling about the country, taking his needs to the people.

"Tuskegee must have new dormitories, a modern laundry, and a veterinary hospital," he had declared from many platforms.

This was all too true. As Washington rolled by the Boys' Trade Building he scrutinized it carefully to see how work on the new wing was progressing. Beyond lay the fine, new Agricultural Building. The U. S. Secretary of Agriculture had attended its dedication that spring. But now the thought occurred to Washington that the building should have been larger. From the parade ground on his right came the loud bark of a sergeant as lines of sweating rookies wheeled and turned in formation. Under a commandant and corps of officers each male student was quickly transformed into a proud, straight cadet whose smart uniform was the envy of every boy in his home town.

"Mr. Washington's back!" The word sped through the buildings and about the grounds. Every boy tightened his belt. Teachers and students quickly checked the tasks at hand. It was well known that the principal might appear anywhere at any moment. He received daily reports from the school, no matter where he was.

Inside his office Washington greeted his secretary as casually as if he had only been for a stroll about the grounds.

"It's ten o'clock, Mr. Scott. We have half an hour before I speak to the conference."

"Yes, Mr. Washington. The conference has its biggest registration ever."

Washington walked to a window and looked down the slope dotted with every conceivable kind of vehicle from old surreys to ox carts. He smiled.

"Some of them have come long distances," he commented.

"We have delegates from every Southern state, besides hundreds of teachers and school principals." Emmett Scott's eyes were anxious. He knew that Washington had been going night

157

and day for weeks on end. He ought to rest. He added reluctantly, "There are several newspapermen and magazine writers from up North, also. They want to interview you. I can furnish them with material, if you'd like, sir."

Washington flipped open his watch. "I'll see them at two o'clock. Now, Mr. Scott, what do you have for me?"

The secretary hid his concern as he opened a folder of letters. Emmett J. Scott had been editing a newspaper in Houston, Texas, when he heard of Booker T. Washington and his work. Still a young man, he gave up what might have become a brilliant newspaper career to serve the man whom he admired and honored above all other men. Emmett Scott's devotion, loyalty, and shrewd wisdom were to prove Washington's strongest prop when the burden seemed more than any one man could carry.

By eleven o'clock of that July morning, Washington was answering questions and asking a few in his annual Tuskegee Negro Conference. He had established this conference in 1891 for the purpose of reaching older people in country districts throughout the state. He started by inviting farmers and their wives in the immediate locality to spend a day at Tuskegee reporting on conditions in their community in order that the school might learn how best to teach them to help themselves. Now rural people came from all parts of the state. They told "Mistah Washin'ton" their troubles and he asked them such simple questions as "How often do you feed your chickens?" and "Do you grow beans in your garden?"

That evening, dinner was spread for all the conference guests on long tables under the trees and Washington went from one table to another eating, drinking lemonade, and talking with his people—the people whom he understood and who loved and understood him. Once Washington caught a glimpse of his daughter, Portia, who with other girl students in their neat blue uniforms was serving the guests. But not until much later that night did the principal see his wife, the third Mrs. Washington.

For a long time after Olivia's death the only mother his children had was a teacher or an officer, a matron or gardener or student. They were bright, likable youngsters: Portia, with her small, piquant face and Fannie's beautiful eyes; inquisitive Booker T., Jr., and little Ernest Davidson. They knew no life other than this institutional one and they made the most of it. Each time their father encountered one of them he sighed heavily and his face wrinkled into a frown.

It was said that Portia implored her father to marry the lovely new lady principal. Margaret James Murray, a native of Mississippi, came to Tuskegee Institute in the autumn following her graduation from Fisk University in Nashville, Tennessee. Though she was highly recommended, Washington reluctantly placed her in charge of the Normal School. Miss Murray had been educated in a "classical college" largely staffed and sponsored by Oberlin College of Ohio. Washington doubted Miss Murray's value to Tuskegee. Much to the principal's surprise, the young lady went about her work with skill and understanding. Her ideals and vision matched Washington's practical experience. Through her efforts a medical dispensary was established in the hamlet adjoining the Institute grounds, a resident physician was added to the faculty, and two small buildings were set up as hospitals for men and women respectively. She reached out from the school and worked among the women and children in the surrounding communities. Now Miss Murray was Washington's wife and the mother of his children, though she retained her position as lady principal.

Though Washington kept his eye on every section of the institution, which now had close to twelve thousand students, his money-raising efforts consumed two-thirds of his time and perhaps more of his strength and energy. He used the platform as well as the press to keep his work before the public. As Tuskegee's program was enlarged the need for money increased. There was no end to the one or the other. Washington's secretary now traveled with him to keep the principal in constant touch with the school, to write individual letters to parents and isolated farmers, as well as to carry on an exhaustive correspondence with hundreds of organizations who wanted Booker T. Washington and to arrange Washington's visits to wealthy philanthropists throughout the country.

In the spring of 1899 friends of the Negro in Boston planned an affair "in aid of Tuskegee," presenting an unusual array of Negro talent. The Hampton Quartette was invited to sing. Washington reached Boston to discover that his fellow speakers were the gifted young Paul Laurence Dunbar, whose lyrical poetry had taken the country by storm, and the erudite Dr. W. E. B. Du Bois, born and reared in Massachusetts, who had been educated in the leading universities of this country and of Europe.

For a moment the recent years faded away and the "head of Tuskegee" was just the "boy from Malden," uneasy, abashed, unsure of himself.

"I'm tired—tired," the man whispered to himself as he hesitated in the wings of the Hillis Street Theatre. He shrank from facing this audience in cultured Boston; he dreaded comparison between himself and the two younger men.

While he tortured himself, the audience, made up of the best people of Boston, white and Negro, waited to hear him. The two other speakers were equally eager. These two, who had never personally known slavery, were happy to give whatever assistance they could to the great work being done at Tuskegee. They had only the deepest appreciation of Booker T. Washington.

The voices of the Hampton Quartette blended in song; Paul Laurence Dunbar read several of his poems; the first address was delivered. Then the audience leaned forward to hear the chief speaker of the evening.

Washington came forward with Du Bois' precise, beautifully rendered English echoing in his ears. For once, the round of applause did not buoy him up and animate his words. The usual ready, apt flow was damned up in the backwash of his mind. His words of greeting were labored; witty stories eluded him; the rich store of Negro folk lore seemed depleted. He managed to impart a few facts about Tuskegee, told something of its increased enrollment, and stated its pressing needs. Then he sat down, lonely and sick at heart.

While the Hampton Quartette sang again, people in the audience murmured that Booker T. Washington looked worn out.

"And no wonder," whispered a sponsor of the affair. "He's going night and day without rest."

At the close of the evening one elegant little lady, known in Boston for her good works, came forward to shake Washington's hand, and asked, "Mr. Washington, have you ever been to Europe?"

Washington had a wild impulse to laugh. He controlled the nervous fluttering in his throat, smiled, and said gravely, "No, ma'am." Then his lips twitched. "What would I be doing in Europe?"

"I think a trip to Europe would be good for you," declared the little lady briskly.

Boston papers were kind. The bare facts about Tuskegee made good copy. Washington read good accounts of his visit, a substantial sum of money was added to Tuskegee's account, and the whole affair was pushed out of his mind.

The letter from the "Boston Committee" reached Tuskegee two weeks later. Friends of Mr. Washington, it said, had raised a sum of money sufficient to pay all the expenses of three or four months in Europe for Mr. Washington and his wife. It added with emphasis that Mr. Washington must have this vacation. The money would be turned over for no other purpose. Emmett Scott's eyes danced when he handed the letter to his chief.

"A trip to Europe is the very best vacation for you, sir!" he said.

"But how can *I* leave Tuskegee?" Washington's gray eyes were baffled.

The answer came in three parts: a second group of friends were pledged to raise sufficient money to keep the school in operation while he was away; Mr. Warren Logan, Secretary-Treasurer of Tuskegee, was thoroughly experienced in running the institution during the principal's long absences; Dr. George Washington Carver, whom Washington had recently taken from the faculty of Iowa State College, was quietly and efficiently bringing the Agricultural Department to a level which did not require Washington's supervision.

The whole thing seemed incredible. "That money would

161

equip the Canning Factory! We need—"

"The money cannot be used to equip the Canning Factory," Scott interrupted gently. "Nor for anything else except this trip. You, sir, need a vacation."

Washington told his wife. Her amazement matched his. Margaret Murray had been reared by a Quaker family. In times of excitement she was apt to lapse into the speech of her childhood. Now she exclaimed, "Thee must be mistaken, Mr. Washington—not to *Europe*! What would people say?"

Washington smiled at this. Together they went over the letter and, as they read, husband and wife began to realize what these weeks could mean. They had scarcely had time to get acquainted, had seldom sat down to a meal together, had never enjoyed a quiet evening alone. A warm flush spread over the face of Tuskegee's lady principal.

"It would be like a—honeymoon," she said softly. "A honeymoon in Europe."

Portia, who was studying in Framingham, Massachusetts, came to New York to see them off. The crowd on the pier that May morning was a gay one.

"We've arranged for friends to look after you in every port," they told the still rather bemused Washington. He smiled, shook hands; accepted letters of introduction, a gift from two generous ladies who wanted to help with the "new Girls' Dormitory"; tried to realize that this was not a dream. He marveled at his wife's happy assurance. Margaret Murray was radiant.

So, on the steamer *Friesland,* the "boy from Malden" set out for distant lands. He was vastly surprised to find that captain and passengers knew who he was and deferred to his wishes. He recorded the fact that "there were not a few Southern men and women on board, and they were as cordial as those from other parts of the country." When the excitement of departure had worn away he began to rest.

It was such an unusual feeling to wake up in the morning and realize that I had no engagements; did not have to take a train at a certain hour; did not have an appointment to meet someone, or to make an address, at a certain hour. How different all this was from experiences I have been through when traveling, when I have sometimes slept in three different beds in a single night!"

After ten days of perfect weather they landed at the old city of Antwerp, in Belgium. They were met and carried off to a hotel facing the public square. From the window of their room they could see people coming in from the country with all kinds of flowers to sell, women in dog carts loaded with large, brightly polished cans of milk, people streaming into the great, Gothic cathedral on the opposite side of the square.

"We're in Europe, Booker T.," Margaret Murray murmured, and slipped her hand through the crook in his arm.

Holland; the Hague, where a Peace Conference was in session; Brussels . . . then Paris!

Hardly had they settled in their Paris hotel when an invitation arrived from the University Club asking Washington to be a guest speaker at a banquet soon to be given there. Among the guests that evening was a former President of the United States, Benjamin Harrison. Washington was introduced by the American Ambassador, who presided at the banquet. Later the Ambassador gave a reception at his residence for Washington and his wife.

While in Paris they saw a good deal of the artist Henry O. Tanner, whom they had known at home. In his *Up from Slavery* Washington writes:

When we told some Americans that we were going to the Luxembourg Palace to see a painting by an American Negro, it was hard to convince them that a Negro had been so honored. I do not believe they were really convinced of the fact until they saw the picture for themselves. My acquaintance with Mr. Tanner reenforced the truth which I am constantly trying to impress upon our students at Tuskegee—and on our people throughout the country—that any man, regardless of color, will be recognized and rewarded just in proportion as he learns to do

163

something well—learns to do it better than someone else —however great or humble the thing may be.

But the climax of the trip was reached in London. Parliament was in session and the London social season was at its height. The Washingtons were flooded with invitations. After much urging Washington consented to attend one large public meeting. It was held at Exeter Hall and here also Washington was introduced by the American Ambassador. The English people hailed Washington as the successor to the great Frederick Douglass, whom they had known and honored. Mrs. Washington spoke at the Women's Liberal Club in Bristol and, later, before the International Congress of Women, then in session in London.

On a lovely afternoon in July a small but distinguished party sailed up the Thames River to Windsor Castle. The Grand Old Lady of England, most revered sovereign of three generations, living quietly far from the noise and bustle of the city, had made known her desire to see London's most talked-about visitor.

Washington stood in the bow of the barge and watched the massive battlements of ancient kings emerge from the surrounding green. He walked under trees planted by hands long since turned to dust, and mounted a staircase worn by the feet of the world's most powerful rulers.

The Queen was not seated on a golden throne, nor did a jeweled diadem adorn the small white head. Yet Washington held his breath while Lady Aberdeen dropped into a low curtsy before the carved armchair. He heard his name spoken in low, deferential tones. He came forward with lowered eyes and bowed before Victoria, by the Grace of God, of the United Kingdom of Great Britain and Ireland, Queen, Defender of the Faith, Empress of India!

Queen Victoria smiled, extended her hand to the ex-slave, and said, "Come closer, Mr. Washington, and tell me about your school. I believe you funny Americans call it Tus-ke-gee."

Sometime later a liveried footman handed him a cup of tea. From the other side of the room, Margaret Murray saw the brown hand tremble as he raised the cup to his lips. The gray eyes sought hers and she saw that, like a little boy's, they were filled with wonder. Suddenly Margaret Murray's eyes misted with tears.

14

Dinner at the White House

It had been a big day at Tuskegee—a triumphant day. As the school year of 1901 started, Tuskegee Institute dedicated its fine new library—gift of Andrew Carnegie. The great man himself came with a full retinue of attendants, riding in his private car. By eight o'clock that morning special trains had brought other notable guests who rolled from the station to the school through streets decorated with flags and bunting. The town of Tuskegee assumed a holiday air. People rushed out to cheer the Governor of Alabama. Long before noon crowds were streaming through the high grilled gates, the band was playing, and the gay apparel of the visitors mingled with the trim, neat uniforms of the students.

Booker T. Washington dropped heavily into the chair in front of his desk. For a moment he closed his eyes. It was nearly midnight. The ground superintendent had made his rounds and the high gate was locked. The last remaining guest was tucked away in the comfortable, attractive guest house. An exhausted student body had gone to bed, as well as its large corps of much-complimented teachers. The only light showing in the Administration Building was the one over the principal's desk.

He was grateful for the stillness, for in his ears still lingered the gay, martial strains of the band as his straight cadets marched in parade. Standing beside him on the reviewing

165

stand, Andrew Carnegie had chuckled with delight. He heard a visiting general tell Tuskegee's commandant, "A fine lot of young men you got there, Major. A fine lot!"

Everything had gone well. When shown the library, Mr. Carnegie could not believe that so much had been done with his gift of twenty thousand dollars.

"You must know that our students did all the work, Mr. Carnegie," Washington explained, "the brickmaking, masonry, carpentry."

Andrew Carnegie nodded his head. His eyes crinkled. "Let me know when you have another pressing need. I can think of no better investment than Tuskegee Institute and you, Dr. Washington."

Remembering, Washington smiled. Dartmouth College had conferred a doctorate upon him the preceding June. The title still embarrassed him, though he wore it with dignity. The years had not stooped or fattened him. The gray hairs at his temples only added distinction to a firm face, unwrinkled except for the fine lines about the eyes. His chin had a more stubborn set than in his youth, but his gray eyes were still level and wide.

Now Dr. Washington rubbed his hand across his eyes in a gesture which was becoming more and more frequent, and hitched his chair forward. On the desk lay a neat pile of papers which he must go through before retiring. He started as his eyes fixed on the top letter. He read the one sheet quickly:

> Buffalo, New York, Sept. 14, 1901—My dear Mr. Washington, I write you at once to say that to my deep regret my visit South must now be given up. When are you coming North? I must see you as soon as possible. I want to talk over the question of possible appointments in the South exactly on the lines of our last conversation together. I hope that my visit to Tuskegee is merely deferred for a short season. Faithfully yours . . .

The letter was signed by the man who only two days before had taken the oath of office as President of the United States— Theodore Roosevelt!

Washington's first reaction was dismayed anger. Why hadn't he been handed this letter at once? What was Emmett Scott thinking of to leave a letter from the President lying on his desk all day?

He half rose from his chair, muttering, "I'll get him over here at once! Good heavens, this is awful!"

The shadows about the big room rebuked him. At what moment during the day could his secretary have approached him with a letter? And why was he so perturbed? This communication did not call for an immediate response. Mr. Roosevelt was asking when he was coming North. Well, when *was* he going North again? He settled back in his seat and covered his eyes with one hand. The letter did not call for an immediate answer. It was, however, cause for reflection.

Vice-President Roosevelt had been elevated to the Presidency because an assassin's bullet had killed President McKinley. Washington felt again the horror he had experienced when the shocking news flashed over the country. President McKinley with several members of his Cabinet had visited Tuskegee two years before. He had been in this very room. Indeed, had sat in this very chair at Washington's desk.

"What shall we do about your Southland, Mr. Washington?" McKinley had asked.

The principal of Tuskegee did not have answers ready. His job was Tuskegee. He had left the running of the country to those in office.

But tonight, with the new President's letter before him, Booker T. Washington pulled up short and considered his course. Long ago he had turned his back on politics. "While politicians talk, I'll work," he had said. He advised other Negroes to "let white folks have their politics; you buy a farm!" From platforms and through the press he had declared, "Skilled workmen, home owners, producers, men and women who ardently and cheerfully contribute to our country's well-being will share all the benefits along with everybody else, regardless of race or color."

This was what he believed—and so he had labored. His people called him "Moses—our Moses!" And they had followed him gladly. There could be no doubt that, in the twenty years since he had started Tuskegee, Negroes had made tremendous progress. Less than forty years out of slavery, over half of them could read and write—they owned 150,000,000 dollars' worth of property!

Yet even now, right here in Alabama, his own state, where the progress of Negroes was so evident, the state which each year sent out hundreds of well-trained, capable, upright young Negroes—here, in Alabama, legislation was being written to disfranchise all Negroes. And Alabama was only following the precedent already established in Mississippi, South Carolina, Louisiana, and North Carolina. Throughout the South, laws were being enacted stripping his people of citizenship, depriving them of all the privileges of decent, civilized living for which Washington was so zealously preparing them.

A groan escaped through the hard-pressed lips and Washington lifted his head. Hollow footsteps sounded in the corridor. Perhaps the night watchman was going through the empty building.

Washington responded to the light knock on his door with, "Come in!"

It was his brother, John, now Superintendent of Industries at the Institute.

"I saw your light and knew you were in here working. Booker T., you're killing yourself! I had to come in and make you go to bed—if that's possible."

John smiled apologetically, but his eyes were anxious. Washington regarded him somberly.

"Don't worry about me, John. I've scarcely been in here all day. This desk—there are matters I—" He gestured vaguely toward the papers.

"Why do you still work so hard, Booker? If you don't have enough help, get more! Good Lord, man, you've already done more than twenty other men manage to do in a whole lifetime. Ease up a bit. You're on top of the world! There's a limit to what any one should try to do."

Booker T. sighed. "Oh, John, John! There's so much left undone—so many loopholes to plug—so much waste in all our efforts." He looked down at his hands as though studying them, and added, "It's so easy to make mistakes."

John laid a hand on his brother's arm. "What's the matter, Booker? What's wrong?"

"The equation isn't working out. I'm not getting the right answers." He smiled quizzically and shook his head. "I never was very good at algebra."

"What on earth do you mean?"

Instead of answering the question, Dr. Washington asked, "What would you think, John, if I told you I was going into politics?"

Half an hour later the two brothers walked across the grounds in the moonlight.

As they parted at a turn in the lane, John said earnestly, "Nothing can dim the value of your work, Booker. You started at the beginning. Whatever you do now is more effective because of what you've already done."

Booker walked on alone to the neat cottage set aside for the principal. His brother's words brought comfort and confidence. His people needed him. He must not fail them.

In the days which followed, Washington scrutinized the newspapers more carefully than had been his habit. He visited the statehouse in Montgomery, chatted with the doorman and one of the porters. He called on several prominent people, then caused a wave of excitement by strolling through the Negro district and dropping into a barbershop.

"Can I get a shave?" he asked casually.

"Hit's Mistah Washin'ton!" The whisper sped all along the street.

The barber tried to shoo the loiterers away until Washington said pleasantly, "Leave them alone, sir, unless they disturb you. I'm rather anxious to know how things are going with folks around here. Perhaps some of you men will tell me."

They pushed forward to tell him.

Early in October, Dr. Washington sent Emmett Scott to Washington with a specific recommendation to President Roosevelt for the appointment of "the Judge of the Middle

169

District of Alabama." He described his candidate as being a "clean, pure man in every respect" and said, "He stood up in the Constitutional Convention and elsewhere for a fair election law, opposed lynching and has been outspoken for the education of both races."

Theodore Roosevelt appointed the man recommended by Booker T. Washington in spite of the fact that he had been an outspoken supporter of William J. Bryan, the Democratic candidate for President.

This precedent-breaking appointment of a Southern Democrat by a Republican President upset the federal officeholding traditions throughout the country. Southern Republicans resented the encroachment upon what they considered as their patronage rights. Somehow it leaked out that the appointment had been made on Booker T. Washington's recommendation. Democrats who had been enthusiastic now questioned the wisdom of allowing a Negro to have an advisory voice in political matters, even when the Negro was the "understanding" Booker T. Washington. Criticism in the South grew so insistent that the Judge found himself in an uncomfortable position.

Neither the President nor Washington seemed unduly disturbed. The Judge was a white man. Washington wanted to move on to the more thorny problem of appointing Negroes to political positions in the South. After further exchange of letters President Roosevelt asked Washington to come to the White House to discuss appointments and "other matters of mutual interest."

There was a new spring in Washington's step, a new ring in his voice. The head of Tuskegee had lifted his sights. There was no slackening in his determination to send out good teachers, able farmers, and skilled workmen—but this was not enough. The Negro could not escape his responsibility for *good government*. To be sure, some risk was involved; but Washington set out for his conference with the President with a high-mounting enthusiasm for this new role.

Washington never wrestled with the perplexing question as to whether or not he could find hotel accommodations. In every city and town there were scores of homes where it was considered an honor to entertain him. On arriving in the capital he went immediately to the home of Benjamin Whitney, a friend since that winter at Wayland Seminary. Whitney had eventually gone into the postal service and settled in Washington.

"Come in, come in, Booker T." Whitney himself opened the door. "My wife is horrified because I didn't meet you. You know you didn't say what train you were taking."

Washington laughed. Years slipped away as he said, "I wasn't sure what time I'd get away. I might have arrived at midnight."

"Well, you're here in good time for dinner. How well you look!"

Washington's arrival anywhere was the signal for a rush of people to see him. This time he had bound his friend to secrecy. He wanted no publicity for his visit with President Roosevelt.

The evening in his friend's home was blissfully undisturbed. Only the family gathered round and plied him with questions about Paris and London. He enjoyed talking about his trip, and time passed unnoticed.

"What a great man you've become!" Whitney's eyes regarded him with something akin to awe. Then his lips twitched. "Nobody at Wayland could have imagined that one day all the world would know—"

"That slow-witted seminary student!" Washington's eyes danced as he finished the sentence.

Mrs. Whitney gasped, but the two men looked at each other and grinned.

"Wasn't it your hat I wore to the reception?" asked Washington.

The friend nodded. For the enlightenment of the wife and two charming daughters, Washington recounted how he had gone to the White House twenty-three years before.

His reception at the White House the next morning was very different. The President received him at once and, turning to his secretary, he said, "There's nothing until the delegation arrives at eleven-thirty, is there, Mr. Loeb?"

"That's right, Mr. President. You have no other appointments."

"Fine!" He rubbed his hands together. "Now then, Dr. Washington, let's talk things over!"

Theodore Roosevelt intended to get things done. He had been an active politician since the day he graduated from Harvard—even before that, some folks said. He had served as Civil Service Commissioner under President Harrison, as Assistant Secretary of the Navy, and as Governor of New York before he became Vice-President. His "Rough Riders" had made him a hero of the Spanish-American War. He had managed to capture the imagination of Negroes throughout the country. Every black boy knew that, when Teddy Roosevelt led his Rough Riders in the charge up San Juan Hill, Negro soldiers had supported the attack. Roosevelt was turning to Booker T. Washington now because conditions in the South worried him. Here was a vast area which in many respects was going to waste. Washington had proved that he knew something about retrieving wasted, castoff material. "I was bent upon making the Government the most efficient possible instrument in helping the people of the United States to better themselves in every way, politically, socially, and industrially," Roosevelt wrote in his *Autobiography,* and the words sound curiously like Booker T. Washington's.

It is not surprising, therefore, that their hour together passed very quickly. When Mr. Loeb appeared and announced "The delegation is here, sir," the President looked up and exclaimed, "Impossible! We've only just begun!"

"It's eleven-thirty, sir," said the secretary softly.

Washington rose at once. But Mr. Roosevelt sat drumming on his desk, a frown on his face.

"When do you have to leave, Dr. Washington?"

"I'm speaking in Pittsburgh tomorrow night, sir."

"Then, by George, you'll have to dine with us tonight." He glanced quickly at the pad on his desk. "Yes, that would do very well. Spencer and Brown will be here and they can broaden the base of our discussion. Will that fit into your travel schedule, Doctor?"

172

"I'll be happy to come. I planned to take the midnight train."

"That settles it!" The President's face beamed as he extended his hand. "Good-bye, then, until this evening, at seven-thirty."

Not until Washington was walking out onto Pennsylvania Avenue did the full import of the President's casual invitation strike him. Then he blinked.

No one in the White House gave any evidence of knowing that a history-making event was being enacted that evening. Mrs. Roosevelt greeted their dark-skinned guest graciously. She asked him questions about Tuskegee. Miss Roosevelt was more interested in his impressions of Holland.

"One of my grandfathers, several times removed, came from Holland," she said. "I've always wondered what it would be like to go back."

The other guests had known that Washington was coming and showed no surprise. One of them asked if it was true that the Negro race was dying out.

Not until after dinner, over brandy and cigars, did the four men get down to serious discussion. Then they considered, one by one, individual Negro officeholders throughout the country, appraised applicants for office, and affirmed the "desirability of having in all offices men whose first concern would be the administration of justice—men whom we could be sure would affirmatively protect the law-abiding Negro's right to life, liberty, and property just exactly as they protected the rights of law-abiding white men." President Roosevelt wanted to know about the public service in the South, so far as the representatives of the federal administration were concerned.

It was a pleasant evening, constructive and productive, Washington thought as he boarded the train that night.

"I think I'm doing very well as a politician," he murmured as he dropped off to sleep.

The next day Negroes in Washington saw Booker T. Washington's name listed in a routine White House news item. They whispered among themselves, hardly believing what they read.

Five days later, when Dr. Washington reached Atlanta,

Georgia, the dinner had become front-page news!

For weeks thereafter it seemed that the South rose up, to a man, to denounce the one upon whom it had lavished its gift. Booker T. Washington had betrayed its most sacred tradition! He who had so stoutly claimed a separate area of achievement for himself, had now taken unto himself the most complete "social equality." He had sat down to dinner with a white man *and his wife*! The fact that the white man in the case was the President of the United States was only incidental. For his part, the President was execrated by every Southern newspaper for having invited a black man to dine with him. It meant nothing that the guest was their own Booker T. Washington.

The articles were all highly emotional. Reporters besieged the President, who would not discuss the matter. They swarmed over Tuskegee. But Dr. Washington would issue no statement. Threatening letters were received by both the President and Washington. The President had the Secret Service to protect him. Tuskegee surrounded its principal with every precaution possible. But for days the campus resembled a camp alerted for danger.

Some voices were raised in defense, some in ridicule. Europeans had trouble making head or tail of the matter. With his characteristic dry humor Washington tells a story which illustrates the wild, illogical aspects of some people's minds. A few weeks after his dinner with President Roosevelt he was traveling through Florida. At a little station near Gainesville, he writes in his *My Larger Education*:

> A white man got aboard the train, whose dress and manner indicated that he was from the class of small farmers in that part of the country. He shook hands with me very cordially, and said, "I am mighty glad to see you. I have heard about you and I have been wanting to meet you for a long while." Of course I was pleased at this cordial reception, but I was surprised when, after looking me over, he remarked, "Say, you are a great man. You are the greatest man in this country." I protested mildly; but he insisted, shaking his hand and repeating, "Yes, sir, the

greatest man in this country." Finally I asked him what he had against President Roosevelt, telling him that, in my opinion, the President of the United States was the greatest man in the country. "Huh! Roosevelt?" he replied with considerable emphasis. "I used to think that Roosevelt was a great man until he ate dinner with you. That settled him for me."

The furor made Booker T. Washington notorious and it enlarged his popularity. People who had criticized his "softness" now admired his "spunk." Northern Negroes rallied to his defense as never before and, when it became evident that the Democrats would use "the Booker T. Washington dinner" to defeat Theodore Roosevelt in the 1904 election, Negroes placed themselves squarely in Roosevelt's corner.

Dr. Washington did not campaign for President Roosevelt, but by the spring of 1904 it became clear to Republicans that every successful appearance of Tuskegee's head was a boost for Roosevelt. Washington's cross-country tours drew tremendous crowds; Tuskegee's funds piled up. That spring Andrew Carnegie turned over 600,000 dollars' worth of U. S. Steel bonds to Tuskegee's endowment fund with one condition: "the revenue of one hundred and fifty thousand of these bonds is to be subject to Booker Washington's order to be used by him first for his wants and those of his family during his life or the life of his widow. . . . I wish that great and good man to be free from pecuniary cares that he may devote himself wholly to his great Mission."

Yet it is probable that the happiest event of that year for Washington was Theodore Roosevelt's triumphant election. On November 10, 1904, two days after the election, he wrote the President the following letter, marked "Personal":

My dear Mr. President: I cannot find words in which to express my feeling regarding the tremendous outcome of Tuesday's election. . . . The result shows that the great heart of the American people beats true and is in the direction of fair play for all, regardless of race or color.

175

. . . I know that you will not misunderstand me when I say I share the feeling of triumph and added responsibility that must animate your soul at the present time because of the personal abuse heaped upon you on account of myself. The great victory and vindication does not make me feel boastful or vainglorious, but very humble, and gives me more faith in humanity and makes me more determined to work harder in the interest of all our people of both races regardless of race or color. The election shows to what a great height you have lifted the character of American citizenship. God keep you and bless you. Yours most sincerely, Booker T. Washington.

◇◇◇◇◇◇◇◇◇◇◇◇◇◇◇◇◇ 15 ◇◇◇◇◇◇◇◇◇◇◇◇◇◇◇◇◇

"For My People"

"Harvard University was not as rich after living two hundred years among the people of Massachusetts as Tuskegee is today, after having lived twenty-five years among the people of Alabama. The oldest and now largest American institution of learning was more than two hundred years arriving at the possession of much less land, fewer buildings and a smaller quick capital than Tuskegee has come to possess in twenty-five years."

This declaration was made by Dr. Charles W. Eliot, President of Harvard University, at the ceremonies commemorating the twenty-fifth anniversary of the founding of Tuskegee Institute.

Booker T. Washington looked over the heads of the vast audience in search of one little old man. Then he remembered that a special place had been prepared for him at the far end of the platform. He turned and smiled into the eyes of Lewis

176

Adams, who had held an umbrella over him that day of his "grand opening"! Today on the platform with him sat a score of men and women whose names were symbolic of the wealth and influence of the nation. Before him were thousands of eager, lifted faces.

Tuskegee Institute now had a resident student population of between fifteen hundred and two thousand boys and girls, with a teaching force of two hundred men and women. It enrolled in its courses from thirty-five hundred to four thousand persons, while its extension school, directed by Thomas J. Campbell, carried instruction to thousands more. The head of Tuskegee's Agricultural Department, Dr. George Washington Carver, was attracting attention by his methods of reclaiming the soil and making use of common materials. The South was turning to him for help, which he gladly gave. The Institute was in continuous session throughout the year. Trades and industries were kept in operation for the benefit of the summer school conducted for teachers.

The school was organized with military precision. No one had any time to waste. A critical eye was kept on academic classes to see that they were correlating their work with trade work. Dr. Washington had a way of leisurely strolling about, day or night, into classroom, shop, or laboratory with a stenographer at his elbow. One new teacher showed this note to a friend:

> Mr. ————: After a visit to your class yesterday, I want to suggest that you get into close contact with some of the teachers here like Mrs. Jones of the Children's House, and Mrs. Ferguson, head of the Division of Education, and Mr. Whiting of the Division of Mathematics, who understand our methods of teaching. Your work yesterday was very far from satisfactory, not based upon a single human experience or human activity. [Signed] Booker T. Washington, Principal.

"He's a hard taskmaster," complained the new teacher.
"He's always just," explained the friend, who had been at

Tuskegee for ten years, "and he drives nobody as hard as he does himself."

Everybody knew that the principal rose at dawn and went, first, to visit his poultry and pigs. None of the other animals 'interested him as did the pigs. He kept fine Berkshires and Polish Chinas for breeding.

"The pig is the most important animal to my people," he would tell visitors. "They eat it from snout to tail. It gives them the most for what they are able to give it." Then he was likely to add softly, "I had a little pig when I was a boy— that I loved." He insisted that the Institute's herd of swine be kept up to its full strength in spite of protests that it was unprofitable to keep so large a herd.

After a hasty breakfast Dr. Washington mounted his horse and rode over the farms and truck gardens, as well as about the grounds inspecting dormitories and shops. By eight o'clock he went to his office and attacked the huge stack of morning mail.

He had recently taken on another responsibility—that of writing for an impatient publisher.

After much probing and urging he had finally agreed to write the story of his life for serial publication in *The Outlook*. His first hesitant efforts produced only three and one-half pages of typewritten material, which he mailed with an apology to the editors. The letter of congratulation and approval which came from them was encouraging, and in spite of his heavy schedule he pushed ahead. Much of the story he dragged from his tired brain while waiting in railway stations or hotels, and during ten- or fifteen-minute intervals snatched in his office. He jotted it down on odds and ends of paper, which were collected and put in order by his secretary. It was physically impossible for him to give adequate time and attention to this writing and he felt apologetic about the product.

The enthusiastic reception of his story by the editors and later by the public amazed and gratified him. *Up from Slavery* brought Washington a new kind of acclaim.

Said William Dean Howells in the *North American Review:* "What strikes you first and last is his constant common sense.

He has lived heroic poetry, and he can, therefore, afford to talk simple prose."

Before Washington's death this book sold one hundred and ten thousand copies in this country alone, was widely read in England, and was translated into French, Spanish, German, Hindustani, and Braille.

Characteristically Dr. Washington regarded the wide distribution of his book as another means of getting his work before the world: "The world sees my people through me, they see my people in me, they will recognize my people as they recognize me."

This was his passion and so he drove himself to further efforts. He gathered around him skilled young writers; he pulled together speeches, plans, notes, blueprints; he dictated and organized materials; he revised what his assistants wrote. The result was other books in quick succession—*The Future of the American Negro, Working with the Hands,* and *My Larger Education*—as well as articles which appeared in *The Atlantic Monthly, The Outlook, The Century Magazine.*

In 1900 Washington founded the National Negro Business League. By 1910 the National League had six hundred local leagues with a membership of forty thousand representing every branch and variety of business, trade, and finance. Dr. Washington was national president and presided over annual conferences held in such centers as Chicago, New York, Dallas, and St. Louis.

When a bill to disfranchise Negroes was introduced in the legislature of Georgia, Washington issued an earnest plea through the columns of the Atlanta *Constitution:*

I cannot think that there is any large number of white people in the South who are so ignorant or so poor that they cannot get education and property enough to enable them to stand the test by the side of the Negro in these respects. It is unfair to blame the Negro for not preparing himself for citizenship and then, when he does get education and property, to pass a law that can be so operated as to prevent him from being a citizen, though he may be a large taxpayer. Southern white people have reached the point where they can afford to be just and generous; where there will be nothing to hide and nothing to explain. Greatness, generosity, statesmanship are shown in stimulating initiative, encouraging every individual in the body politic to make of himself the most useful, intelligent, and patriotic citizen possible."

With the passage of the disfranchising bill in the Georgia state legislature the ballot for Negroes virtually disappeared from the South.

Then in the summer of 1911 a particularly vicious lynching in Alabama was flashed over the wires. Washington was torn between sticking to the educational work which he believed would, in the end, remove all conditions conducive to lynching and the demands of Northern Negroes to "bring the murderers to justice."

On a hot July afternoon, shortly after addressing the large assembly of the summer school then in session, the principal collapsed in his office.

He revived quickly and shooed away secretaries and stenographers, insisting in an irritable voice, "I'm quite all right—quite all right. For a moment—the heat—bothered me. That's all!"

Emmett Scott, however, went for Mrs. Washington, who sent for the doctor. Both Mrs. Washington and the doctor then insisted that the principal should at least take the rest of the day off, go home, and lie down.

"Don't be a fool!" snapped Washington, shaking off the doctor's hand. Then, suddenly, a surprised look flashed across his face; he put his hand to his side and whispered, "I've got a pain."

They got him home and put him to bed. After a cursory examination, the doctor gave him a powder and said, "Now you'll go to sleep, sir. And I'll wager that's the best thing in the world for you."

Outside, the doctor said to Mrs. Washington, "Perhaps he's just exhausted. At the moment I can't be sure. But of this I am certain: you'll have to make him take a vacation. Otherwise, madam, our little hospital is going to take in its most illustrious patient."

Washington felt fine the next day. The early morning was pleasantly cool. He laughed ruefully and said, "Guess I did need a good sleep!"

Margaret Murray suggested that he make a long-anticipated trip to Denmark.

"Here's your chance to study those agricultural methods you've been reading about." She clinched her argument by adding, "Think what it will mean to our work here."

He traveled with only a secretary this time. But he was received in Denmark like visiting royalty. Of his presentation to the King of Denmark he wrote later in the *New York Age:*

> I had not been talking with the King many minutes before I found that he was perfectly familiar with the work of Tuskegee; that he had read much that I had written, and was well acquainted with all that I was trying to do for the Negroes in the South. He referred to the fact that Denmark was interested in the colored people in their own colony in the Danish West Indies, and that both he and the Queen were anxious that something be done for the colored people in the Danish possessions similar to what we were doing at Tuskegee. He hoped that I would find it possible to visit the Danish West Indies. As the interview was closing, the King took me by the hand and said, "The Queen would be pleased to have you dine at the palace tonight," at the same time naming the hour.

Dr. Washington had been so cordially and informally received that he forgot to back out of the room as he had been instructed to do. Later that evening at the summer palace, about ten minutes' drive from Copenhagen, Washington discovered that the Queen also spoke English perfectly and was happy to know that he intended to export Danish methods to Tuskegee.

He returned home looking rested and in excellent spirits.

But as the months sped by and he resumed the same strenuous schedule, he was conscious of increasing weariness. Nevertheless there was so much to do. There was no time to rest.

"My people need me more each day," he whispered. And he began to despair because he felt he was accomplishing so little.

Emmett Scott was now Secretary-Treasurer of the Institute and Booker T. Washington began shifting more and more responsibility upon the younger man's shoulders—not that he might rest but that he might be free to go on to something else. He became more critical and more demanding of all those around him.

"We must get this work done!" he said sternly.

Since he slept very little anyhow, he went to bed later and got up earlier. His morning ride sometimes was extended to some lonely farm where he would surprise the farmer and his wife, inquire into their well being, give them advice. He never missed a speaking engagement, sometimes appearing in two places on the same evening; he visited Negro schools and presided over conferences.

The sharp pain struck him one night while he lay in a Pullman berth. He sat up gasping for breath as the train swayed and rumbled along through the darkness. He put out his hand to ring for the porter.

No! he whispered. If word went through the train that Booker T. Washington was ill, the situation would become intolerable. He did not want to answer questions—he did not want to start speculation. *It will go away in a minute.* The pain did subside and after a while he lay back on the pillow.

He did not, however, go to sleep. For now he must face something he had been trying to keep out of his mind. He tried to marshal his thoughts—to take some account.

His eldest son, Booker T., Jr., was teaching on the Institute faculty, Ernest was away studying medicine. Daughter Portia was happily married. He smiled—good, all good. His brother, John, was doing a fine job at Tuskegee; his adopted brother, James, was a postmaster. He could be proud of them all. And

182

with what dignity and grace his wife, Margaret Murray, worked by his side!

"How good life has been to me!" he murmured. "No man has ever had so much good fortune as I!"

A long, shuddering sigh shook him. Not yet could he face the thought of leaving so much work undone!

"Time! Oh, God," he prayed, "a little more time."

As if in answer to his prayer, it was several months before the pain struck again. And in those months Washington worked as only a powerful, determined man can work when he knows that his time is limited.

"What would you do, Mr. Scott," he asked one day, "if I should go away for a—long time?"

Scott looked at him sharply; his eyes probed deep into the face where fine wrinkles were beginning to show.

"What you have set up here, Dr. Washington, is no longer dependent on our puny strength. It will survive regardless of what I or any other individual does or does not do. This school is a symbol of your great service to our people, and that service will continue as long as our people need it."

"Thank you, Mr. Scott," said Washington, turning away. "Thank you very much."

On October the twenty-third Dr. Washington left Tuskegee to attend the annual meeting of the American Missionary Association at New Haven, Connecticut. On the evening of the twenty-fifth he delivered an address in Woolsey Hall at Yale University, after which he took a late train to New York.

He was ill when he arrived in New York. Friends prevailed upon him to go to St. Luke's Hospital for a thorough examination. Specialists declared that the sick man was suffering from nervous exhaustion and from arteriosclerosis.

"I suggest," said Dr. Bastedo, "that you send for Mrs. Washington at once."

Washington asked to see his friends and told them, "I believe I am dying, my friends, and I want to get back to Tuskegee at once. This is my last request to you: help me to get back—among—my people!"

"Is he strong enough to travel?" they asked fearfully.

The doctor shook his head. "I don't think that it matters. I should advise that you do as he wishes."

Every comfort was provided for the long trip south, but Booker T. Washington was unconscious during most of the trip. He knew when they reached Chehaw.

"Almost home," he whispered, "almost home."

Emmett Scott's face seemed distinct to him in the shadows. His eyes cleared and he said quietly, "I've been called Moses—Moses, leading his people." He smiled. "A good name for me. I did go to them—I did my best. But like that other Moses—I have not been able to lead my people to the—Promised Land. . . . Still a long—way—to go."

It was dusk as his carriage rolled through Tuskegee's gates. He insisted on sitting up. He returned the somewhat faltering salute of the cadet. For the news had preceded him and the students huddled together speaking in whispers.

"It's good to be back," he murmured. "This is where I belong."

He died shortly before sunrise on the morning of November 14, 1915.

Booker Taliaferro Washington needed no eulogies. They came from every part of the country, written in newspapers across the land. They came from over the waters—from the great and the little people of the earth.

The dusty Alabama roads were filled with people making their way to Tuskegee to see "Mistah Washin'ton" for the last time. Into each one he had poured some part of himself. These were his People who now altogether made up his Everlasting Life.

And Tuskegee Institute was there—each red brick building sharp against the sky—a monument to him. The broad fields filled now with ripened grain, the orchards heavy with fruit, the cattle on the hills—all were monuments to him.

It was the time of harvest—the time when the sheaves are cut and bound and stored away. This was the time when they laid the "boy from Malden," the Modern Moses, to rest in his Good Land.

Bibliography

Armstrong, Mrs. M. F. and Ludlow, Helen W. *Hampton and Its Students*. New York: G. P. Putnam's Sons, 1874

Bond, Horace Mann. *Negro Education in Alabama*. Washington, D. C.: The Associated Publishers, Inc., 1939

Du Bois, W. E. Burghardt. *Souls of Black Folk*. Chicago: A. C. McClurg & Co., 1903

Studies of the Negro Problems. Atlanta University Press, 1906

Moton, Robert R. *Finding a Way Out*. Garden City, N. Y.: Doubleday, Page & Co., 1920

Riley, B. F. *The Life and Times of Booker T. Washington*. London and New York: Fleming H. Revell Co., 1916

Scott, Emmett J. and Stowe, Lyman Beecher. *Booker T. Washington, Builder of a Civilization*. Garden City, N. Y.: Doubleday, Page & Co., 1916

Washington, Booker T. *The Future of the American Negro*. Boston: Small, Maynard & Co., 1902

My Larger Education. Garden City, N. Y.: Doubleday, Page & Co., 1911

Up from Slavery. An Autobiography. Garden City, N. Y.: Doubleday, Page & Co., 1901

Working with the Hands. Garden City, N. Y.: Doubleday, Page & Co., 1904

Washington, Booker T. and Du Bois, W. E. Burghardt. *The American Negro*. London: T. Fisher Unwin, 1909

Washington, E. Davidson, edited by. *Selected Speeches of Booker T. Washington*. Garden City, N. Y.: Doubleday, Doran & Co., 1932

Twenty-Two Years' Work of Hampton Normal and Agricultural Institute. Records of Negro and Indian Graduates. Hampton School Press, 1893

Index

Douglass, Frederick, 81-82, 106, 109, 110-111, 113, 156, 164
Du Bois, W. E. B., 156, 160
Dunbar, Paul Laurence, 160

Eliot, Charles W., 154, 176
Emancipation Proclamation, 13, 17
Exeter Hall, 164

Fenner, Mr., 129
Fisk University, 159
Fort Marian, Florida, 117
Fortress Monroe, 71, 80
Framingham, Massachusetts, 137
Freedmen's Bureau, 48, 77
Future of the American Negro, The, 179

Gainesville, Florida, 174
Granny Lou, 13, 30-32
Great Kanawha River, valley of, 32, 38
Greek, 105-107

Hague, The, Holland, 163
Hampton Institute. *See* Hampton Normal and Agricultural Institute
Hampton Normal and Agricultural Institute, 58-59, 62, 64-66, 71-76, 77, 78-83, 84, 87-89, 90-91, 93, 95, 98, 104, 105-106, 107, 111, 114-118, 119-125, 127-130, 138, 149-150
Hampton Roads, 59, 78
Harrison, Benjamin, 163
Harvard University, 154, 176
Hawaiian Islands, 76
Hayes, Presdent Rutherford B., 105, 109, 110-111, 124

Hemenway, Mrs. Mary, 137-138
Hillis Street Theatre, 160
Hampton Quartette, 160
Houston, Texas, 158
Howard University, 107, 108, 113
Howe, Mr. (teacher of agriculture at Hampton), 78
Howells, William Dean, 178
Huntington, West Virginia, 112

International Congress of Women, 164
Iowa State College, 161

James River, 73, 78, 80
Jamestown, Virginia, 80
Jefferson, Thomas, 108
Johnson, Reverend, 47-48, 56-57, 68, 80, 86-90, 92, 96, 100-103, 104, 111, 147

K.K.K. *See* Ku Klux Klan
King of Denmark, 181
Ku Klux Klan, 98-101, 112

Larry, John (teacher in charge of printing room at Hampton), 80-83, 115
Latin, 105-107
Lincoln, Abraham, 13, 16, 17, 28
Lockwood, Reverend C. L., 71-72
Lodge, Henry Cabot, 154
Logan, Warren (Secretary-Treasurer of Tuskegee), 161
London, England, 164
Lord, Miss Nathalie (teacher of reading at Hampton), 80
Lynchburg, Virginia, 83

McKinley, President, 167

187

188

About the Author

SHIRLEY GRAHAM was born in Indiana, the daughter of a Methodist minister, and raised in parsonages all over the country. In high school she was elected class poet and her essay on Booker T. Washington took first place for literary distinction. She has studied at the Sorbonne in Paris and at Oberlin College in Ohio where she took her Master's Degree. In 1938 she was awarded a Julius Rosenwald Fellowship for Creative Writing, and in 1947 she received a Guggenheim Fellowship. Miss Graham travels around the world a great deal, but she makes Brooklyn, New York, her home.